BRITISH LABOUR STRUGGLES:
CONTEMPORARY PAMPHLETS 1727-1850

ROBERT OWEN AT NEW LANARK

Two Booklets and One Pamphlet

1824-1838

Arno Press

A New York Times Company/New York 1972

Reprint Edition 1972 by Arno Press Inc.

Reprinted from copies in the Kress Library
Graduate School of Business Administration,
Harvard University

BRITISH LABOUR STRUGGLES: CONTEMPORARY PAMPHLETS 1727-1850
ISBN for complete set: 0-405-04410-0

See last pages for complete listing.

Manufactured in the United States of America

Library of Congress Cataloging in Publication Data
Main entry under title:

Robert Owen at New Lanark.

    (British labour struggles:
contemporary pamphlets 1727-1850)
    Reprint of An outline of the system of education
at New Lanark, by R. D. Owen, first published 1824;
of The fundamental principles of the New Lanark
system exposed, by W. M'Gavin, first published 1824;
and of Mr. Owen's establishment at New Lanark, a
failure!! By E. Baines, first published 1838.
    1. New Lanark Establishment. 2. Owen, Robert,
1771-1858. I. Owen, Robert Dale, 1801-1877. An
outline of the system of education at New Lanark.
1972. II. M'Gavin, William, 1773-1832. The
fundamental principles of the New Lanark system exposed. 1972. III. Baines, Edward, 1800-1890. Mr.
Owen's establishment at New Lanark, a failure!! 1972.
IV. Series.
HX696.O9R62   335'.12   72-2543
ISBN 0-405-04435-6

Contents

AN OUTLINE

OF

THE SYSTEM

OF

EDUCATION

AT

NEW LANARK.

By ROBERT DALE OWEN.

GLASGOW:

Printed at the University Press,

FOR WARDLAW & CUNNINGHAME, GLASGOW;

BELL & BRADFUTE, EDINBURGH; AND

LONGMAN, HURST, REES, ORME, BROWN, & GREEN,

LONDON.

1824.

DEDICATION.

_____

To ROBERT OWEN, Esq.

I DEDICATE this my first production to you, my
dear Father, because I trace the formation of a
great part of my own character, and the origin of
a great part of my own feelings and sentiments to
yourself.

In teaching me to think, you led me to examine
principles, intimately connected with the best
interests of mankind; and I feel that I have derived
both pleasure and profit from the examination.

I have seen these principles partially applied to practice, and have witnessed the many beneficial effects which were produced. I have seen their application counteracted by many opposing circumstances, whose influence in rendering the experiment incomplete, had been predicted and explained by the principles themselves.

And it gives me pleasure to know that you are about to commence a more perfect experiment, where practice may uniformly accord with principle; because I believe this to be necessary to prove to the world, that your principles are indeed founded in fact and in true religion.

But its success will scarcely create in my own mind a stronger conviction than I already entertain, of the certainty and facility, with which poverty and vice and misery may be gradually removed from the world.

R. D. OWEN.

INTRODUCTION.

THE system of education which has been introduced at New Lanark, differs essentially
from any that has been adopted in a similar
institution in the United Kingdom, or, probably, in any other part of the world.

Some particulars regarding it, may, therefore, prove interesting, as exhibiting the
results produced on the young mind, by
combinations, many of them new, and almost
all modified by the general principles on
which the system is founded.

It may be necessary to premise, that, the
experiment which has been here instituted
for the purpose of ascertaining the capabilities of the human mind, at a very early
period of life, cannot, by any means, be
considered as a full and complete, but, on

the contrary, as merely a partial and imperfect one ; and the results thence obtained, however satisfactory, not as those which a system of training, rational and consistent throughout, may be expected to produce, but only as a proof—an encouraging one, it is presumed—of what may be effected even by a distant approximation to it, under the counteraction of numerous prejudices and retarding causes.

The difficulties and disadvantages, incidental to an experiment of this nature, will be most correctly estimated by those, who may have had an opportunity of witnessing the introduction of any new system, however beneficial ; and the pertinacity with which old established habits and ideas continue to hold out against apparently self-evident improvements.

Such individuals will give to the following considerations their due weight :

That, as the children lodge with their parents, and remain in school during five hours only, each day, the counteracting influence of an association with persons who have not received a similar education, must be very great, particularly as those persons, whether parents, relations, or elder companions, are such as, from their age and experience, the children generally look up to with respect, and whose habits and manners they are but too apt to adopt implicitly as a model for their own.

That the difficulty was very great in procuring teachers, who, to the requisite fund of knowledge, general and particular, should unite all the various qualifications of habits, and of temper, so essential in a teacher of youth ; unaccompanied too with any pedantry, which might prevent him from regarding his pupils in the light of younger friends, or conversing familiarly with them, and entering into their ideas, or even sometimes into their little projects and amusements, or which might disincline him to be himself, when necessary, instructed and directed.

That, as the parents in general avail themselves of the permission which is granted them, to send their children into the manufactory at ten years of age, the education of these children, being thus broken off at the most interesting and important period, generally remains incomplete ; for, although the schools are open in the evening for the instruction of those older children who are employed in the works, yet many do not attend regularly, and it is found that those who do, cannot, after ten hours and a half of labour, apply in the same manner, or derive, by any means, the same benefit from that instruction, as the day scholars.

That many of the children, previously to their admission into the schools, had been permitted to acquire bad habits and improper dispositions, an acquisition which is frequently made, to a great extent, before the little creatures have reached the age of two years, and which most parents, under existing circumstances, have neither the knowledge, nor the means, to prevent. And lastly,

That several of the arrangements, necessary to the completion of the system, are yet only in progress, and that many more remain to be introduced.

NEW LANARK, }
Oct. 1823. }

AN OUTLINE,

&c.

It will be proper, before proceeding to details, to state the general principles by which these schools are regulated.

The children are governed, not by severity, but by kindness; and excited, not by distinctions, but by creating in them a wish to learn what they are to be taught.

All rewards and punishments whatever, except such as Nature herself has provided, and which it is fortunately impossible, under any system, to do away with, are sedulously excluded, as being equally unjust in themselves, and prejudicial in their effects.

Unjust—as, on the one hand loading those individuals with supposed advantages and distinctions, whom Providence, either in the formation of their talents and dispositions, or

B

in the character of their parents and associates, seems already to have favoured; and on the other, as inflicting farther pain on those, whom less fortunate, or less favourable circumstances, have already formed into weak, vicious, or ignorant,—or in other words, into unhappy beings.

And prejudicial—in rendering a strong, bold character, either proud and overbearing, or vindictive and deceitful; or in instilling into the young mind, if more timid and less decided, either an overweening opinion of its own abilities and endowments, or a dispiriting idea of its own incompetency—such an idea as creates a sullen, hopeless despondency, and destroys that elasticity of spirit, from whence many of our best actions proceed, but which is lost as soon as the individual feels himself sunk, mentally or morally, below his companions, disgraced by punishment, and treated with neglect or contempt by those around him.

It may be a question, which of these two motives, reward or punishment, is in its ultimate effects upon the human character, the more prejudicial, and produces the greater unhappiness; the one in generating pride, vanity, inordinate ambition, and all their concomitant irrational and injurious feelings and passions, or the other in debasing the character, and destroying the energies of the individual. And, in this view, the advocates for such a system might perhaps with some plausibility support its *justice*, by arguing—"that the apparent advantages and distinctions, bestowed on already favoured individuals, often cause them more unhappiness and dissatisfaction, than all the mortifications and disappointments of their seemingly less fortunate companions; and thus tend to equalize the amount of positive advantages acquired by each." But surely such an argument is but a poor defence of the system. It is only supporting its justice at the expense of its expediency.

We have said, that all rewards and punishments were excluded from these schools, except those which nature herself has established. By *natural* rewards and punishments, we mean the *necessary consequences*, immediate and remote, which result from any action.

If happiness be " our being's end and aim,"
and if that which promotes the great end of
our being be right, and that which has a contrary tendency be wrong,—then have we obtained a simple and intelligible definition of
right and wrong. It is this : " *Whatever,
in its ultimate consequences, increases the happiness of the community, is right ; and whatever, on the other hand, tends to diminish that
happiness, is wrong*." A proposition, at once
clear in itself, and encouraging in its application ; and one which will scarcely be rejected but by those who are unaccustomed
to take a comprehensive view of any subject,
or whose minds, misled and confused, perhaps, by words without meaning, mistake the
means for the *end*, and give to those means
an importance, which is due to them only in
as far as they conduce to the end itself, the
great object of all our pursuits, and the secret mainspring of all our actions.

Every action whatever must, on this principle, be followed by its natural reward and
punishment ; and a clear knowledge and
distinct conviction of the necessary consequences of any particular line of conduct, is

all that is necessary, however sceptical some
may be on this point, to direct the child in
the way he should go; provided common
justice be done to him in regard to the other
circumstances, which surround him in infancy and childhood. We must carefully
impress on his mind, how intimately connected his *own* happiness is, with that of *the
community*. And the task is by no means
difficult. Nature, after the first impression,
has almost rendered it a sinecure. She will
herself confirm the impression, and fix it in-
delibly on the youthful mind. Her rewards
will confer increasing pleasure, and yet
create neither pride nor envy. Her punishments will prove ever watchful monitors;
but they will neither dispirit nor discourage.
Man is a social being. The pleasures resulting from the exercise of sincerity and of
kindness, of an obliging, generous disposition, of modesty and of charity, will form,
in his mind, such a striking and ever-present
contrast to the consequences of hypocrisy
and ill-nature, of a disobliging, selfish temper,
and of a proud, intemperate, intolerant
spirit, that he will be induced to consider

the conduct of that individual as little short of insanity, who would hesitate, in any one instance, which course to pursue. He would expect, what appeared to him so self-evident, to be so to every one else; and feeling himself so irresistibly impelled in the course he followed, and deriving from it, daily and hourly, new gratification, he must be at a loss to conceive, what could have blinded the eyes, and perverted the understanding of one who was pursuing, with the greatest difficulty and danger to himself, an opposite course, pregnant with mortification in its progress, and disappointment in its issue; employing all his powers to increase his own misery, and throwing from him true, genuine happiness, to grasp for the hundredth time, some momentary gratification, if that deserve the name, which he knew by experience would but leave him more dissatisfied and miserable than it found him.

And his surprise would be very natural, if he were not furnished with the clew, which can alone unravel what appears so palpably inconsistent with the first dictates of human nature. That clew would enable him to trace the origin of such inconsistency to the system of education at present pursued, generally speaking, over the world. Artificial rewards and punishments are introduced ; and the child's notions of right and wrong are so confused *by the substitution of these, for the natural consequences resulting from his conduct,*—his mind is, in most cases, so thoroughly imbued with the uncharitable notion, that whatever he has been taught to consider wrong, deserves immediate punishment ; and that he himself is treated unjustly, unless rewarded for what he believes to be right ;—that it were next to a miracle, if his mind did not become more or less irrational : or if he chose a course, which, otherwise, would have appeared too self-evidently beneficial to be rejected.

The principles that regulate the instruction at New Lanark, preclude any such ideas. A child who acts improperly, is not considered an object of *blame*, but of *pity*. His instructors are aware, that a practical knowledge of the effects of his conduct is all that is required, in order to induce him to change it. And this knowledge they endeavour to

give him. They show him the intimate, inseparable, and immediate connection of his
own happiness, with that of those around
him ; a principle which, to an unbiased
mind, requires only a fair statement to make
it evident ; and the practical observance of
which, confers too much pleasure to be
abandoned for a less generous or more selfish course.

In cases where admonition is necessary, it
is given in the spirit of kindness and of
charity, as from the more experienced, to
the less experienced. The former, having
been taught wherein true self-interest consists, are aware, that had the individual who
has just been acting improperly, had the
knowledge and the power given him, to
form his character, he would, *to a certainty*,
have excluded from its composition such
feelings, as those in which his offence origi-
nated ; because that knowledge would have
informed him, that these were only calculated to diminish his own happiness. The presence of those feelings would constitute the
surest proof, that the knowledge and the
power had been denied him.

Such, at least, would be the inference we should deduce from similar conduct, in any parallel case. Let us suppose a traveller anxious to reach the end of his journey. He is young and inexperienced, and perfectly unacquainted with the country through which he is to pass. Two roads are before him : the one is smooth and pleasant, affording, at every turn, some new and animating prospect ; it leads directly to his object ; if he follow it, he will every where meet with agreeable and intelligent companions, all travelling in the same direction, and all anxious to give him every information and assistance. The other, though at first not uninviting, soon becomes dangerous and rugged, leading through a bleak, waste country, the prospect on every side dismal and discouraging ; he who pursues it will be continually beset by thieves and assassins ; he must be prepared, in-every individual he meets, to discover a rival or an enemy; all his fellow-travellers will conceive it to be their interest to mislead and perplex him ; for they know that the inns are few, and small and ill supplied, and that every additional companion lessens the chance of adequate accommodation for themselves : this road, too, dangerous and difficult and disagreeable as it is, gradually changes its direction ; it will lead the unfortunate traveller, if indeed he survive its perils and hardships, farther and farther from the object of his destination, and will at last probably conduct him into a strange, barbarous country, where he will sit down in despair, fatigued and harassed, dissatisfied with himself, displeased with his fellow-creatures, disgusted with his journey, and equally afraid and unwilling either to proceed, or to return.

Our traveller, however, chooses this latter path in preference to the other. Now, can we suppose it a possible case, that, at the time he did so, he knew what he was choosing. It is admitted that he *had* a choice, and that he chose evil, and rejected good. But should we therefore assume that he *himself created the preference which gave rise to that choice ;* that he *wilfully formed an erroneous judgment ;* and that he merited pain and punishment by such perversity ? Should we

not rather conclude, either that he had decided at random, unconscious of the importance of his choice, or had been deceived by
a casual review of the general appearance of
the country? Could we avoid remarking,
that circumstances which he had not created, and which he could neither alter nor regulate, induced a preference, and thus determined his choice? And if we attempted to
put him into the right path, would our language be that of anger or violence? Should
we consider it necessary to employ any *artificial* inducements in urging him to change
his course? or should we not rather conclude, that this would only lead him to suspect our disinterestedness, and confirm him
in the resolution he had already adopted?
Nay, if, to ensure his safety and comfort,
we proceeded to actual force, and obliged
him to take the other path, is it not but too
probable, that, as soon as he was relieved of
our troublesome presence, he would strike
into the first cross-road that presented itself,
to return to his original course? How much
more easily would the proposed end be effected by a simple dispassionate statement of

facts, unaccompanied by violence, and unattended by any artificial inducement! How much more wise would be our conduct if we endeavoured to procure a map of the country, and to prove to the traveller the accuracy of the information we gave; or if we advised him to enquire of those who might be returning from the road he had been so anxious to follow, whether *they* had found it a pleasant or a direct one. They would at once tell him the real state of the case. We might then endeavour to induce him to accompany us in the other direction, only requiring of him that he should look, and hear, and judge for himself.

Now, I believe it to be impossible, that, with even a moderate knowledge of human nature, we should not be able to prove to this traveller, young and inexperienced, and uninformed as he is, our sincerity in the advice we had given him; and I am equally certain, that if we did so, and he believed our statement, he *could* not *deliberately make himself miserable, in preference to making himself happy ;* otherwise the desire of happiness cannot be a universal law of our nature.

In the case just stated, the traveller is supposed to commence his journey alone. If he were accompanied by many companions of his own age, and if they all struck into the opposite road, we admit it to be possible that advice and even conviction might be inefficient to prevent him from going along with them. Man is gregarious; and he might choose to traverse a desert in the company of others, though it led to danger and to death, in preference to beginning a *solitary* journey, though it conducted through gardens to a paradise. But, on the other hand, if his companions followed the road to happiness, it would scarcely be necessary to warn *him* of the danger of separating from them and choosing the other path. If, indeed, *example* and *advice* proved equally unavailing in inducing him to accept of happiness, then nothing less than insanity would account for his conduct; and even in such a case, violence or artificial inducements would prove ineffectual.

We might safely build on a rock, and yet we prefer a bank of sand, artificially supported on all sides, with infinite trouble and

anxiety and expense, and which, in all likeli-
hood, the first flood will carry along with it!

Let us suppose a set of children, overawed
by the fear of punishment, and stimulated
by the hope of reward, kept, which is but
seldom the case, during the presence of their
teachers in what is called " trim order," apparently all diligence and submission ; will
these children, we ask, when the teacher's
back is turned, and this artificial stimulus
ceases to operate, continue to exhibit the
same appearance? or are they not much
more likely to glory in an opportunity of
running into the opposite extreme, and
thereby exonerating themselves of a restraint so irksome? Nay, more : impressed
as they are with the idea that pleasure and
duty run counter to each other, and that,
therefore, rewards and punishments are employed to induce them to follow duty at the
expense of pleasure, can we expect that such
individuals should in after life hesitate to
reap present gratification from any line of
conduct, not immediately followed by artificial punishment? for that is a *criterion of
right and wrong*, which had been brought

home to their feelings in too forcible a manner to be quickly forgotten, or easily effaced. Can we wonder that so few individuals leave our schools with other impressions than these? If we do, we surely forget that the law of cause and effect applies equally in the formation of the human character, as in that of a blade of grass or any other natural production.

It is scarcely necessary to allude to the difference which will be found in the character of those, who have never felt these artificial excitements, and whose *youthful* actions have been regulated by a principle, which will operate equally *in after life*. *They* will know that virtue always conducts to happiness, and that vice leads only to misery; and therefore, they will follow virtue from its own excellence, and avoid vice from its own deformity.

Obstinacy and wilfulness are often fostered, even in generous minds, by a feeling of independence, in rejecting what is attempted to be forced upon them. And public opinion confirms this feeling. He obtains, among his school-fellows, the character of a brave, spirited fellow, who will set himself—whether right or wrong—against the will of their mutual tyrant, for that is the light in which they are too often obliged to regard their instructors. In an institution, conducted on correct principles, the scene is reversed. No credit is obtained, where no risk is incurred. Public opinion is against those who refuse obedience to, or elude commands, which, it is known, are never given but on a reasonable occasion, or enforced, but in a mild and gentle manner. *Obedience* is never confounded with *cowardice*, and therefore obedience is popular. The most generous and intelligent individuals uniformly lead their companions, and these are gained, when they see themselves treated in a generous and intelligent manner. No party is formed against the authority of the teachers; for even a schoolboy's generosity will not oppose force to mildness, or determined obstinacy to uniform kindness. The teachers are loved, not feared, yet without any deduction from their authority, whenever they find it necessary to exert it. Their pupils converse with them out of school hours, or even during the lessons, when it can be done with propriety, with the most perfect ease and freedom, and such conversation is regarded as a privilege. In the New Lanark institution, this practice has already led to questions and remarks from the children themselves, which would be considered far above their years, and than which nothing can be a greater proof of the good effects of this system of instruction.

What the children have to learn, is conveyed to them in as pleasant and agreeable a manner as can be devised. The subject is selected, and treated with a view to interest them as much as possible. In the lectures, to which we shall presently have occasion to allude, if the interest or attention is observed to flag, the teacher looks to *the lecture itself,* and to his *manner of delivering it,* rather than *to the children,* to discover the cause. It is on this principle, that sensible signs and conversation are made the medium of instruction, whenever it is practicable ; and this plan, dictated by nature, has been found to be eminently useful.

Their attention is never confined too long

c

to one object : a lesson for the day scholars, in any particular branch, never exceeding three quarters of an hour.

No unnecessary restraint is imposed on the children ; but, on the contrary, every liberty is allowed them, consistently with good order, and attention to the exercise in which they may be engaged.

By a steady adherence to such a system, but little difficulty will be experienced, in mildly enforcing whatever has once been required of the scholars ; even in cases where they may perceive neither the immediate nor ultimate benefit of a compliance.

These principles are no plausible, unsupported theory. Even as such, they appear conclusive. In the absence of any direct experiment, their consistency with every thing we see around us, and with the first feelings and dictates of our nature, would give them no inconsiderable weight. But an experiment has been made under every disadvantage,—what has been done in school has been counteracted without,—(for most of the parents, as was to be expected, do not yet comprehend the utility of this mode of

3

instruction, and have continued their system of rewards and punishments); the teachers themselves have discovered the practice of the system but by degrees; it has been attacked and denounced even by those who had been connected with it—has been cramped by imperfect arrangements ; and checked by a mixture of the old with the new principles and practices, inseparable from a first trial ;—and yet the result, much as it falls short of what, under different circumstances, might have been obtained, has been, in a very high degree, satisfactory. No such result, as far as we are aware, has hitherto been produced in any similar institution; it is a result, too, which is obtained in the most agreeable manner, both for the instructors and the instructed, without repressing a single generous feeling, and without incurring the risk of abandoning the schoolboy to the world, either as a determined violator of law and of principle, or as a mean, undecided, dispirited character, equally afraid to do wrong, and unwilling to do right.

Having thus adverted to the general principles by which these schools are governed, the full discussion of which might easily be extended to volumes, and is consequently foreign to our present purpose, we proceed to lay before the public an outline of the details of the plan.

The " New Institution," or School, which is open for the instruction of the children and young people connected with the establishment, to the number of about 600*, consists of two stories. The upper story, which is furnished with a double range of windows, one above the other, all round, is divided into two apartments; one, which is the principal school-room, fitted up with desks and forms, on the Lancasterian plan, having a free passage down the centre of the room, is about 90 feet long, 40 feet broad, and 20 feet high. It is surrounded, except

---

* Of these about 300 are day scholars, under ten years of age. The rest are above that age, and attend in the evening when their work is completed; in summer, however, their number is considerably below that here stated.

at one end, where a pulpit stands, with gal-
leries, which are convenient, when this room
is used, as it frequently is, either as a lecture
room or place of worship.

The other apartment, on the second floor,
is of the same width and height as that just
mentioned, but only 49 feet long. The
walls are hung round with representations of
the most striking zoological and mineralogical specimens; including quadrupeds, birds,
fishes, reptiles, insects, shells, minerals, &c.
At one end there is a gallery, adapted for
the purpose of an orchestra, and at the other
are hung very large representations of the
two hemispheres; each separate country, as
well as the various seas, islands, &c. being
differently coloured, but without any names
attached to them. This room is used as a
lecture and ball-room, and it is here, that
the dancing and singing lessons are daily
given. It is likewise occasionally used as a
reading room for some of the classes.

The lower story is divided into three apartments, of nearly equal dimensions, 12 feet
high, and supported by hollow iron pillars,
serving, at the same time, as conductors, in

winter, for heated air, which issues through the floor of the upper story, and by which means the whole building may, with ease, be kept at any required temperature. It is in these three apartments that the younger classes are taught reading, natural history, and geography.

We may here remark, that it is probable, the facility of teaching the older classes particularly, would have been greatly increased, had some part of the building been divided into smaller apartments, appropriating one to each class of from twenty to thirty children, provided such an arrangement had not encroached either on the lecture room, or principal school-room.

Each of the two elder classes for the boys, and the same for the girls, who at that age are taught reading, writing, &c. separately from the boys, and only meet them during the lectures, and in the lessons in singing and dancing, consists of from twenty to forty children. The younger classes, composed indiscriminately of boys and girls, are rather more numerous. A master is appointed to each class. There are likewise, attached to the institution, a master who teaches dancing and singing, a drilling master, and a sewing mistress.

At present the older classes are taught reading, writing, &c. in different parts of the principal school-room, the size of which prevents any confusion from such an arrangement; but, as was before observed, the facility with which their attention could be gained, would probably be greatly increased, could a separate apartment be appropriated to each class. The very size of the room, too, increases the difficulty, of itself no slight one, of modulating the voice in reading.

The hours of attendance, in the day school, are from half past seven till nine, from ten till twelve, and from three till five in the afternoon. In winter, however, instead of coming to school again in the afternoon from three to five, the children remain, with an interval of half an hour, from ten till two o'clock, when they are dismissed for the day; making the same number of hours in summer and in winter.

The ages of the children are from eighteen months to ten or sometimes twelve years.

They are allowed to remain at school as long
as their parents will consent to their doing
so ; though the latter generally avail themselves of the permission which is granted
them, to send their children into the manufactory at ten years of age, or soon after.
It is the wish of the founder of these schools,
that the parents should not require their
children to attend a stated employment till
they are at least twelve years old ; and it
cannot admit of a doubt, that the general
adoption of such a measure would be productive of the most important advantages to
the parents themselves, to the children, and
to society at large.

The infant classes, from two to five
years, remain in school only one half of
the time mentioned as the regular hours of
attendance for the other classes. During
the remainder of the time, they are allowed to amuse themselves at perfect freedom,
in a large paved area in front of the Institution, under the charge of a young woman,
who finds less difficulty—and without harsh-
ness or punishment—in taking charge of,
and rendering contented and happy, one

hundred of these little creatures, than most
individuals, in a similar situation, experience
in conducting a nursery of two or three
children. By this means, these infants acquire healthful and hardy habits; and are,
at the same time, trained to associate in a
kind and friendly manner with their little
companions; thus practically learning the
pleasure to be derived from such conduct,
in opposition to envious bickerings, or ill-
natured disputes.

The school is open in the evening to the
children and young persons, from 10 to 20
years of age; the system pursued with them
is so similar to that adopted in the day
school, that in describing the one, we shall
give an accurate idea of the other also.

The dress worn by the children in the
day school, both boys and girls, is composed
of strong white cotton cloth, of the best
quality that can be procured. It is formed
in the shape of the Roman tunic, and reaches,
in the boys dresses, to the knee, and in those
of the girls, to the ancle. These dresses are
changed three times a week, that they may
be kept perfectly clean and neat.

The parents of the older children pay 3d.
a month for their instruction. Nothing is
paid for the infant classes, or for the evening scholars. This charge is intended merely to prevent them from regarding the Institution with the feelings connected with a
charity school. It does not amount to one-
twentieth part of the expenses of the school,
which is supported by the proprietors of the
establishment.

It has been deemed necessary, in order
to meet the wishes of the parents, to commence teaching the children the elements of
reading, at a very early age; but it is intended that this mode should, ultimately, be
superseded, at least until the age of seven or
eight, by a regular course of natural history,
geography, ancient and modern history,
chemistry, astronomy, &c. on the principle,
that it is following the plan prescribed by
nature, to give a child such particulars as he
can easily be made to understand, concerning the *nature and properties* of the different
objects around him, before we proceed to
teach him the *artificial signs* which have
been adopted to represent these objects. It

is equally impolitic and irrational, at once to disgust him by a method to him obscure or unintelligible, and consequently tedious and uninteresting, of obtaining that knowledge, which may, in the meantime, be agreeably communicated by conversation, and illustrated by sensible signs ; and which may thus, by giving the child a taste for learning, render the attainments of reading and writing really interesting to him, as the means of conferring increased facilities, in acquiring further information.

The following are the branches of instruction at present taught at New Lanark.

READING.

Great difficulty has been experienced, in procuring proper school books for the different classes. Those at present in use, are in many respects defective : they are but ill adapted to the capacities of children so young, and are consequently not calculated to interest them sufficiently. An exception to this last observation must however be made in favour of Miss Edgeworth's little works ; but even these contain too much of

praise and blame, to admit of their being regarded as unexceptionable. From some little
volumes of voyages and travels, too, illustrated by plates and maps, and interspersed
with amusing and characteristic anecdotes,
great assistance has been derived. The elder
classes have often only one copy of each
work, from which one of their number reads
aloud to the others, who are generally ques-
tioned, after a few sentences have been read,
as to the substance of what they have just
heard. In their answers, they are not confined to the author's words; on the contrary,
their answering in a familiar manner, and
employing such expressions, as they themselves best understand, is considered as a
proof, that they have attended more to the
sense, than to the sound.

The general principle, that children should
never be directed to read what they cannot
understand, has been found to be of the
greatest use. The invaluable habit of en-
deavouring to understand what is read or
heard is thus formed. That great and general error, the mistaking of the *means* for the
end, is avoided, and the erroneous idea ex-

cluded, that acquiring a knowledge of the *medium*, through which instruction may be conveyed, is the acquisition of the instruction itself. The children, therefore, after having become acquainted with that medium, will not rest satisfied with this mere mechanical attainment. A knowledge of reading and writing is considered but as furnishing a child with tools, which may be employed for the most useful, or most pernicious purposes, or which may be rusty and unemployed in the possession of him, who having obtained them at great trouble and expense, is yet unacquainted with their real use. The listlessness and indifference so generally complained of by him, whose unpleasant duty it becomes, to force learned, but to them unmeaning sounds, upon his ill-fated pupils, who are thinking of nothing all the time, but the minute that is to free them from the weary task,—are scarcely known under such a system.*

---

* That the system *actually in practice* at New Lanark is imperfect, and consequently incapable of uniformly producing all the results, which would otherwise be obtained—has already been stated.

It is for this reason, that, but for the wishes of the parents, and of parties connected with the establishment, the Scriptures and Church Catechism would not be put into the hands of children, at so early an age as that of the day scholars. There are many parts of the Scriptures, which children of that age should not be made acquainted with, and many more which they cannot understand ; and the Catechism of the Scotch Church is so abstruse and doctrinal, that even their superiors in age and understanding might be puzzled, if called upon to explain, what, as children, they learned to repeat.

The children are taught to read according to the sense, and, as nearly as possible, as they would speak ; so as, at once, to show, that they comprehend what they are reading, and to give their companions an opportunity of comprehending it likewise. In order to teach them the proper tone and modulation of the voice, the master frequently reads to his class some interesting work ; he then allows his pupils to ask any questions, or make any remarks, that may occur to them.

WRITING.

The mode of teaching writing, is, in the commencement, nearly the same as that adopted in most schools; but as soon as the children can write a tolerably fair text copy, the master begins to teach them current hand writing, according to a plan which has been lately adopted in various seminaries. By this method the children write without lines; and with a little attention, soon learn to correct the stiff formal school hand, generally written, into a fair, legible business hand, such as shall be useful to them in after life.

The writing copies consist of short sentences, generally illustrative of some subject connected with history or geography; and the pupils finally proceed to copy from dictation, or from a book or manuscript, any passage that may be considered as difficult, and at the same time important to be retained in their memory. Thus, as soon as possible, applying the newly acquired medium of instruction in the most efficacious manner.

ARITHMETIC

Has hitherto been taught on the system which commonly prevails in Scotland. The elder classes, however, are just beginning a regular course of mental arithmetic, similar to that adapted by M. Pestalozzi of Iverdun in Switzerland. In this, as in every other department of instruction, the pupils are taught to *understand* what they are doing ; the teacher explains to them *why* the different operations, if performed as directed, must be correct ; and in what way the knowledge they are acquiring, may be beneficially employed in after life.

SEWING.

All the girls, except those in the two youngest classes, are taught sewing, including knitting, marking, cutting out, &c. One day of the week is appointed, when they are desired to bring to school any of their garments (which must previously have been washed) that may require mending, and these they are taught to repair as neatly as possible.

NATURAL HISTORY, GEOGRAPHY, AND ANCIENT AND MODERN HISTORY.

These studies are classed together, because, though distinct in themselves, and embracing, each of them, so great a fund of information, they are taught at New Lanark nearly in the same manner; that is to say, in familiar lectures, delivered extempore, by the teachers. These lectures are given in classes of from 40 to 50. The children are subsequently examined regarding what they have heard; by which means the teacher has an opportunity of ascertaining, whether each individual pupil be in possession of the most important part of the lecture which he has attended. In these lectures, material assistance is derived from the use of sensible signs, adapted to the subject, and which we shall explain more particularly in their place. Each master selects a particular branch, and delivers, as has been already stated, a short lecture to 40 or 50 children at once. The

D

number was formerly from 120 to 150 in
one class; but this was found much too large,
and one half or one third of that number is
as many as it is found expedient to assemble
together, except when the lecture is so interesting, as at once to rivet every child's attention, and so easily understood, as to require no subsequent explanation whatever.
The attainment of this very important point,
it may be observed, will require great attention, considerable ability, and a correct
knowledge of human nature. It is extremely difficult for the teacher, particularly if he
has had but little experience in delivering
lectures to children, to preserve the proper
medium between too much and too little detail—to distinguish between unnecessary particulars, which will only divert the attention
from the main subject, and those, which are
absolutely necessary to children, in the way
of explanation. By the former, we refer to
such particulars as relate to abstruse questions, to politics, to uninteresting, tedious
descriptions of particular animals or countries,
especially if these differ but slightly from
each other; to any thing, in short, that is not

6

striking and interesting in itself, or becomes so, as illustrative of some general principle, or characteristic of some leading feature. To the latter will belong such simple and distinct details, as may explain the phenomena of nature, of science, or of civilization, together with such as tend to create enlarged ideas, to repress illiberal or uncharitable sentiments on any subject, or to teach children to value every thing for its real worth, and prevent their being misled by the relation of events, which are too often held up as glorious and praiseworthy, but which, reason teaches us, are equally irrational and injurious to the happiness of the community.

In commencing the exposition of any subject, too great pains cannot be taken to avoid all minor details, and, first of all, to give the pupils a distinct outline of what is to be taught them ; and to impress this so clearly and definitely on their minds, that they shall be enabled to arrange any subsequent details accordingly. This outline should then be only partially filled up, selecting the most important features, and illustrating these by characteristic anecdotes at greater or less length ; than which nothing impresses more distinctly or durably on the mind of a child, the subject to which such anecdote may relate. Subsequently, when further advanced, the pupils may be safely allowed, without fear of perplexing, or overloading their minds, to enter into any important details ; and these they will be able at once to classify and appreciate.*

These are the general principles, which regulate the instruction which is given on such subjects, at New Lanark. We are aware how difficult it frequently proves, to deduce from general principles, their practical application ; but this difficulty, in the present case, experience will gradually remove.

Natural History is taught to all the scholars, even to the youngest, or infant classes ; who can understand and become interested in a few simple particulars regarding such domestic animals as come under their own observation, if these are communicated in a sufficiently familiar manner ; for this, in-

* As a specimen of the manner in which such an outline is communicated to the scholars, see Appendix.

deed, is almost the first knowledge which Nature directs an infant to acquire.

In commencing a course of Natural History, the division of Nature into the Animal, Vegetable, and Mineral Kingdoms, is first explained to them, and in a very short time they learn at once to distinguish to which of these any object which may be presented to them, belongs.* The teacher then proceeds to details of the most interesting objects furnished by each of these kingdoms, including descriptions of quadrupeds, birds, fishes, reptiles, and insects—and of the most interesting botanical and mineralogical specimens. These details are illustrated by representations of the objects, drawn on a large scale, and as correctly as possible. It is desirable, that these representations should be all on the

---

* Even in the course of such simple illustrations, considerable powers of mind may be elicited. In one of the younger classes at New Lanark, to which the teacher had been explaining this division, the pupils were asked to which kingdom the plaster with which the ceiling of the room was covered, belonged. They answered, "To the Mineral Kingdom;" but one little fellow added, "and to the Animal Kingdom too." And on being asked why? he replied, "Because there is hair in it, and that once belonged to an animal."

same scale ; otherwise the child's idea of their relative size becomes incorrect. These drawings may be either hung round the room, or painted, as the botanical representations at New Lanark are, on glazed canvass, which is rolled from one cylinder to another, both cylinders being fixed on an upright frame, at about six or eight feet distance from each other, so as to show only that length of canvass at once. These cylinders are turned by means of a handle, which may be applied to the one, or to the other, as the canvass is to be rolled up or down.

The classes are subsequently, individually, encouraged to repeat what they have heard, to express their opinions on it freely, and to ask any explanation. Such examinations enable the teacher to ascertain, what parts of the lecture have been most suited to the capacities, or calculated to call forth the attention, of the children ; and, on the contrary, what portions were too abstruse and uninteresting to be retained. He is thus daily directed in his choice of materials for future lectures ; and he gradually discovers the extent of the powers of mind which his pupils possess.

In commencing a course of Geography,
the children are taught the form of the earth,
its general divisions into Land and Water, the
subdivisions of the land into four Continents,
and into larger and smaller Islands, that of
the water into Oceans, Seas, Lakes, &c. ;
then the names of the principal countries, and
of their capitals, together with the most striking particulars concerning their external appearance, natural curiosities, manners and
customs, &c. &c. The different countries
are compared with our own, and with each
other.

The minds of the children are thus opened,
and they are prevented from contracting
narrow, exclusive notions, which might lead
them to regard those only as proper objects
of sympathy and interest, who may live in
the same country with themselves—or to
consider that alone as right, which they have
been accustomed to see—or to suppose those
habits and those opinions to be the standard
of truth and of perfection, which the circumstances of their birth and education have
rendered their own. In this manner are
the circumstances, which induce national pe-

culiarities and national vices, exhibited to them; and the question will naturally arise in their minds: "Is it not highly probable that we ourselves, had we lived in such a country, should have escaped neither its peculiarities, nor its vices—that we should have adopted the notions and prejudices there prevalent? in fact is it not evident, that we might have been Cannibals or Hindoos, just as the circumstance of our birth should have placed us, in Hindoostan, where the killing of an animal becomes a heinous crime; or amongst some savage tribe, where to torture a fellow creature, and to feast on his dead body, is accounted a glorious action?" A child who has once felt what the true answer to such a question must be, cannot remain uncharitable or intolerant.

The children acquire a knowledge of the zones, and other artificial divisions of the earth; and it is explained to them, that these are not actual and necessary, but merely imaginary and arbitrary divisions, and that they might have been very different, without in any way altering the real and natural divisions of our globe.

Any one of the older classes at New Lanark, on being told the latitude and longitude
of a place, can at once point it out; can say
in what zone it is situated, and whether
therefore, from its situation, it is a hot or a
cold country—what is the number of degrees
of latitude and longitude between it, and any
other given country, even though on the opposite hemisphere; together, probably, with
other details regarding the country; as for
instance, whether it is fertile, or a desert;
what is the colour and general character, and
what the religion of its inhabitants; what
animals are found there; when, and by whom
it was discovered; what is the shortest way
from England to that country; what is the
name of the capital city, and of the principal
mountains and rivers; and perhaps relate
something of its history, or a variety of characteristic anecdotes which he may have heard
regarding it. They can thus travel, as it
were, over the whole world, taking all the
principal countries in rotation.

In the course of the lectures, numerous
opportunities present themselves to communicate much general information, not strictly

connected with the branches themselves ; as for example, descriptions of natural pheno- mena, of trades, manufactures, &c. Thus, in short, furnishing them with whatever is useful or pleasant, or interesting for them to know.

Ancient and Modern History constitutes another branch of their education. It may be thought, that in teaching History, the aid of sensible signs can be but seldom called in. The reverse, however, is the case. Their application here is, in fact, more complete than in any other branch. Seven large maps or tables, laid out on the principle of the Stream of Time, and which were originally purchased from Miss Whitwell, a lady who formerly conducted a respectable seminary in London—are hung round a spacious room. These, being made of canvass, may be rolled up at pleasure. On the Streams, each of which is differently coloured, and represents a nation, are painted the principal events which occur in the history of those nations. Each century is closed by a horizontal line, drawn across the map. By means of these maps, the children are taught the outlines of

Ancient and Modern History, with ease to
themselves, and without being liable to con-
found different events, or different nations.
On hearing of any two events, for instance,
the child has but to recollect the situation,
on the tables, of the paintings, by which these
are represented, in order to be furnished at
once with their chronological relation to each
other. If the events are cotemporary, he
will instantly perceive it. When the formation and subdivisions of large empires are
represented, the eye seizes the whole at once ;
for wherever the coloured stream of one nation extends over another, on these tables, it
is indicative, either of the subjection of one
of them, or of their union ; and their subsequent separation would be expressed by the
two streams diverging again. The children
can therefore point out the different historical
events, as they do the countries on the map of
the world, count the years and centuries as
they do the degrees of latitude and longitude ;
and acquire an idea almost as clear and tangi-
ble of the history of the world, as that which
the first terrestrial globe they may have seen,
gave them of its form and divisions. We

know, ourselves, how easily we can call to mind any events, representations of which we were, as children, accustomed to see, and we may thence estimate the tenacity with which such early impressions are retained.

The intimate connexion between Natural History, Geography, and History, is evident, so that in lecturing on one of these subjects, the teacher finds many opportunities of recalling to the minds of his pupils various portions of the others.

RELIGION.

The founder of the schools at New Lanark has been accused of bringing up the children without religion.

The direct and obvious tendency of the whole system of education there, most fully warrants, as it appears to us, a representation the very reverse of this; and as much has been asserted, and still more insinuated on the subject, we may be allowed to state our reasons for this opinion.

An acquaintance with the works of the Deity, such as these children acquire, must

lay the basis of true religion. The uniform
consistency of such evidence, all nations,
and all sects, at once acknowledge. No di-
versity of opinion can exist with regard to it.
It is an evidence with which every one who
is really anxious that his children should
adopt a true religion, must wish them to
become acquainted; whether he may have
been born in a Christian country, or be
a disciple of Mahomet, or a follower of
Bramah. Because simple facts can never
mislead, or prejudice the mind. They can
never support a religion which is false ; they
must always support one which is true. He
who hesitates to receive them as the basis of
his religion, tacitly acknowledges its inconsistency. " And where there is inconsistency,
there is error." If the subsequent religious
instruction, which a child is to receive, be
true, then will the instructor derive, in
teaching it, the greatest assistance from the
store of natural facts, which the child has
previously acquired ; because true religion
must be completely in unison with all facts.
If such subsequent instruction be false, then
will it certainly become a difficult task to

induce a belief in its truth, because a child, whose mind has been thus prepared, will probably soon discover, that it is not in accordance with what he knows to be true; but every one must admit the advantage of such a difficulty. Even supposing a child instructed in true religion, and believing it implicitly, without, however, having acquired that belief by deducing its truth from known or well accredited facts,—upon what foundation can such a belief be said to rest? The first sceptic he may converse with, will probably excite a doubt of its truth in his mind; and he himself, being unable to defend his opinions, and having no means of reasoning on the subject, may soon become a violent opposer of that religion, which, though true, had yet been taught to him before he had acquired sufficient knowledge to understand its evidence, or was capable of judging of its truth or falsehood.

This reasoning is peculiarly applicable in the case of any religion, the evidence for which is chiefly derived from historical deductions.

In any other study, the inconsistency of expecting the pupils to deduce correct conclusions before the facts upon which the reasoning proceeds, are known to them, would be glaringly evident. Why then lose sight of this consideration upon a subject so important as religion?

If a chemist were anxious that a child should be able to trace and understand some valuable and important deductions, which with great study and much patient investigation, he had derived from certain chemical facts; would he act wisely in insisting that the child should at once commit to memory, and implicitly believe these deductions? Would he act consistently in objecting to a system, which should first teach the pupil the elements of chemistry, should gradually store his mind with chemical facts, and at length, when his judgment had become matured, place before him these important deductions, and allow him to judge for himself, as to their accuracy?

What should we think of a professor of chemistry, who should object to such a plan? Who would join with him in stigmatizing, as an infidel in the great principles of chemistry, or in denouncing as an enemy to the science itself, the man who expressed his conviction, that it was irrational, before the child could know any thing of the *elementary principles* of the science, to insist upon its *ultimate deductions?* Would not the chemist, who expressed a fear, that unless these were received and implicitly believed *in infancy,* they would not be received or believed *at all,* excite, by the expression of such an opinion, a suspicion of their truth or accuracy?

And is religion a less important, or a less abstruse science than chemistry? Is it of minor consequence that no such cause should exist for attaching suspicion to the great truths of religion? Or are religious doctrines more easily understood than chemical deductions? Or are they not, perhaps, like these, founded on facts? If they are not, they stand not on a rock, but on a sandy foundation. If they are—as it is presumed they must be—then is a knowledge of these facts a necessary preliminary to the study of the science of religion.

As such, it is communicated to the children in the schools at New Lanark.

And on this principle it is considered, that a child, at an early age, should become acquainted with facts, instead of being instructed in abstruse doctrinal points. If it often requires all the powers of the most matured human reason to decide on these points, surely we do wrong to present any of them to the minds of children. Such a proceeding only serves to puzzle and perplex them: it creates listless and inattentive habits: in most cases, it gives children a decided dislike to the study itself. They learn to regard religion, and every thing connected with it, as gloomy, tiresome and mystical; fit only for those, who have lost all power or opportunity of enjoying any thing else.

It would be a libel on religion to suppose these to be the natural consequences of teaching it to children. They are only the necessary results of forcing on the young mind, the prevalent ideas on this subject. Under a different system a religion of confidence, and peace, and love, and charity, could produce neither fear, nor disgust; nor could it ever become unattractive, if presented to

E

children in a simple and natural light. But, in teaching it, we must not depart from those principles, which regulate the rest of our instruction. We must not expect, that children should like a study, which does not interest them, or should feel interested in a study, which they do not understand. If we do, we shall infallibly meet with the results, which alone, as experience tells us, such a system is calculated to produce. But let us not designate these, either the natural consequences of teaching religion, or evidences of the original corruption of the human heart.

If we plant a healthy vine-shoot in an excellent soil; but if, at the same time, being unacquainted with the proper mode of cultivating vines, we neglect to water it, and surround it with a variety of shrubs, by way of support, which, instead of answering this purpose, cramp the growth of the plant, exclude the sun from it, and render it weak and barren; let us not be surprised at the unhappy results of our management; or conclude that no vines planted in that ground can ever flourish or bear valuable fruit; neither let us libel the soil, by imputing to it original, irremediable barrenness. Let us rather inquire if our treatment of the plant be such as nature dictates, or as, reasoning from analogy, and from our previous knowledge of agriculture, we are warranted in supposing conducive to its successful culture. Otherwise it should cease to be matter of surprise, if we find vines flourishing luxuriantly even in wild, neglected spots, while, under our care, they go to decay, and become but a nuisance and a vexation.

To speak without a metaphor—it is not only a fact, that true religion requires no artificial supports, but it is likewise certain, that by surrounding it with these, we only exclude the light of reason, and render principles suspected, the truth of which, if they had not been thus hidden, and obscured, would long since have established itself on the most solid basis.

Again—we are told, that the heart of man "is deceitful above all things, and desperately wicked." And it is undeniable, that the present character of mankind is neither a sincere nor a virtuous one. Indeed, perfect sincerity would expose its possessor either to ridicule, to hatred, or to the imputation of insanity. And any general character approaching to real virtue could not exist under the chilling influence of the existing arrangements of society. This we must acknowledge, with however much regret. But we must be careful in regard to the conclusions we deduce from the fact. We must weigh the matter well, before we admit, that human nature is *necessarily* thus corrupt under EVERY system—or utterly abandon the idea, that the most noble and superior sentiments, good faith, sincerity, generosity, independence and fortitude, kind and social, and charitable feelings, are its inherent qualities, which require only the influence of a mild and genial climate, to draw them forth—and adopt in its place the gloomy picture, loaded with disgusting defects, and sordid qualities, which is held up to us as a true representation of our nature, and over which we may brood, till fancy herself either discovers, or creates the resemblance. If it be correct, then may we give up all hope of any great or permanent improvement in this world, for the prospect before us is dismal and bleak, and discouraging indeed. It matters not that the intelligence and beneficence of the Creator is conspicuous alike in the instinct, which directs the smallest insect in the way he should go, and in the principle, which regulates and upholds thousands of worlds in empty space. It matters not that every inferior being seems fitted for the condition assigned to it, for man himself, it seems, is not. In his formation, an all-wise and omnipotent Creator has failed. Man's prospects of happiness are indeed fair and promising, but his heart has been made inherently depraved, and must always remain so—and that mars and blasts them all. To attempt its improvement would be in fact to oppose the fiat of his Creator, which has stamped deceit and depravity even on the earliest consciousness of infancy.

In inculcating that religion teaches such a doctrine, let us at least confess to ourselves, that it is one, whose direct tendency is, *to discourage all attempts to promote the virtue or the happiness of the world;* and to fill our mind with vague and painful adprehensions for the future ; on the ground, that an *all-good* and *all-powerful* Being has formed, or (which is the same thing) has permitted to be formed in the heart of man, a principle, *which must render all such attempts abortive,* and *all such apprehensions but too well founded.*

Yet this doctrine, and many others of a similar tendency, form part of the religious instruction which is at present given, even to the youngest children. The world is at issue in regard to many of these doctrines ; yet they are unhesitatingly presented, in the most uninteresting and dogmatical manner, to the mind of an infant, and *he* is expected to comprehend them. Can we wonder, that such a mode of proceeding should bring religion into disrepute, and that instructions, given with a view to elevate and ennoble the mind, should in their ultimate effects, but leave behind them an idea of a Being, infinitely powerful indeed, but agitated by human passions, any thoughts of whom it is wise to banish from the mind, as only calculated to terrify and distress ;— and an uneasy, undefined feeling of mysterious dread, just sufficient to embitter any moments, into which thoughts of religion may intrude.

We act unwisely in adopting a system of religious instruction which shall, in any one instance, have been found to produce such a result.

At New Lanark, every opportunity is embraced of inculcating those practical moral principles which religion enjoins; and of storing the minds of the children, with the most important and striking natural facts; but the consideration of any abstruse doctrines is, as far as the religious views of the parents will admit, reserved for an age, when the pupils shall be better fitted to judge for themselves, and to weigh, with an accuracy, which it would be folly to expect from a child, the opposing arguments that are employed to support or to attack disputed points. By this means, the real interests of truth *must necessarily be promoted;* for it is evident that an individual, whose judgment has been thus informed, must be much less likely to reject truth, or to receive error, than it is

possible for the unprepared mind of an infant to be.

It appears to us, that if an individual be
sincere in his religious profession, whatever
peculiar tenets he may hold, he must, on
mature consideration, approve of the plan,
which is now suggested, as the most certain method of *disseminating his particular
opinions* over the world. And simply because each individual believes his own opinions to be true, or he would not entertain
them.

If it be admitted that a very large ma-
jority of the religions of the world are false
—and it is certain, that only one *can* be true
—then does the admission furnish an additional argument in favour of this mode
of instruction. For it is very unlikely that
any false religion would endure such a
test; and it is certain, that a religion founded
on reason and on truth, must be essentially
promoted by it, to the exclusion of all others.

We shall not enter into any arguments in
support of the doctrines propounded by
Calvin ; nor shall we question their truth
or accuracy : the discussion is irrelevant to

our present purpose; but it appears to us evident to a demonstration, that if these doctrines are true we cannot adopt a more effectual method of inducing the whole world to become Calvinists, than that now recommended. If false, the sooner they are exploded the better.

It is a fair question, whether too little interference in so delicate a subject as that of religion, or too great latitude in religious toleration, can ever exist? That an opposite system has excited the most bitter and violent of all animosities, that it has armed the neighbour against his neighbour, the father against his children, has destroyed the peace and harmony of families and of nations, has deluged the world with blood, and, under the sanction of the most sacred name, countenanced atrocities, during the relation of which we seem to listen to the history, not of men, endowed with reason, but of demons, possessed with an infernal spirit of savage madness—these are facts, which every page of our history must establish. Can we be too tenacious in maintaining a principle, the practical influence of which, is to prevent *the possibility* of their recurrence ?

This is the principle that has always regulated the religious instruction, in the New Lanark Schools. An endeavour has been made to rescue human nature from the imputations thrown upon it by the conduct of individuals, actuated by intemperate religious zeal—a conduct, which has often seemed to justify the strongest expressions regarding human deceit and human depravity. At New Lanark these imputations find no support : in pursuing the system adopted there, no cause of complaint has arisen against the natural depravity of our nature. On the contrary, experience seems completely to warrant the opinion, that our nature is a delightful compound, capable, no doubt, of being formed to deceit and to wickedness, but *inherently* imbued neither with the one nor the other—that if fear be excluded as a motive to action, a child will never become deceitful, for it will scarcely have a motive to deceive.—That if a child be taught in a rational manner, it will itself become rational, and thus, even on the most selfish principle avoid wickedness—and that our only legitimate cause for surprise is the consideration, that human nature, as it now exists, is neither so deceitful nor so wicked as the present arrangements of society would seem calculated to make it.

We should apologize for this digression, but that we feel the importance of the subject, and the necessity that those who would improve and re-form the rising generation, should not create to themselves imaginary difficulties, where no real difficulties exist; and that we have seen how much evil may be done, when a teacher first takes it for granted, that his pupils are all depraved and irrational beings, and then treats them as such. The very tone and manner, which such an idea produces, destroys confidence, and creates distrust and dislike. When confidence is lost and dislike excited, the case becomes indeed hopeless; and the teacher, whatever be his talents, will meet with real and increasing difficulties, and daily discover fresh cause for distrust and vexation. Unjust suspicion first *creates* its object, and then glories in the penetration which *dis-*

covered it. His pupils must consider that
they have no character to lose, and are thus
deprived of a great inducement to virtue.
They will thwart him in all his measures,
and deceive and oppose him on every occasion ; because children will not act gener-
ously, unless they be treated with generosity.

Before concluding this important subject,
it may be necessary to say ; that no allusion
has been made in this place to a fact which
has already been stated ; viz. that the scriptures are and have always been statedly
read, and the catechism regularly taught
there—because this has been done, not as
being considered the proper method of con-
veying religious instruction to the minds
of young children, but because the parents
were believed to wish it; and any encroach-
ment on perfect liberty of conscience, was
regarded as the worst species of tyrannical
assumption.

Besides the studies already mentioned,
the children are instructed in music and

dancing ; which are found essentially to contribute towards moral refinement, and improvement. When properly conducted, each
of these acquirements becomes a pure and
natural source of enjoyment ; and it is a well
authenticated fact, that the best method of
making a people virtuous, is to begin by
rendering their situation comfortable and
happy.

SINGING.

All the children above five or six years of
age are taught singing, sometimes by the
ear, sometimes by the notes. They begin
by learning the names and sounds of the
notes, and by singing the gamut ; then proceed to strike the distances, and finally
acquire such a knowledge of the elements of
the science of music, as they may easily reduce to practice. The musical notes and
signs, as well as a variety of musical exer-
cises, are represented on a large scale, on a
rolled canvass, similar to that on which we
have mentioned, that the botanical specimens are painted. A small selection of sim-

ple airs is made, for the school, every three months. The words to these are printed on sheets, one of which is given to each child. Spirited songs, in the bravura style, are found to be much more adapted to children under ten years of age, than more slow and pathetic airs; into the spirit of which they seldom seem to enter, while the former are uniformly their favourite songs, particularly any lively national airs with merry words. Almost all the children show more or less taste for music; although of course this appears in one child spontaneously, while in another it requires considerable cultivation.

The vocal performers in the evening school are sometimes joined by the instrumental band, belonging to the village. This recurs in general once a week.

DANCING

Is taught, as a pleasant, healthful, natural and social exercise, calculated to improve the carriage and deportment, and to raise the spirits, and increase the cheerfulness and hilarity of those engaged in it. The dances are varied. Scotch reels, country dances, and quadrilles are danced in succession ; and by some of the older pupils with a simple and unaffected ease and elegance, which we have never seen surpassed in children of their age.

Besides dancing, the children, boys and girls, now and then go through a few military evolutions, as well to give them the habit of marching regularly from place to place, as to improve their carriage and manner of walking. This species of exercise is never continued long at a time ; and stiffness and unnecessary restraint are avoided as much as possible; on the principle, already mentioned, and which pervades the whole of the arrangements in these schools, that whatever is likely to prove unpleasant or irksome to the children, and is not necessary for the preservation of good order, or for some other useful purpose, should never be required of them. At the same time, whatever is really necessary to the proper regulation of the school, is uniformly but mildly enforced.

To prevent any confusion or irregularity,

each teacher is furnished with a list of the lessons, which his class is to receive during the week, and these are of course so arranged, that the lessons of the different classes cannot interfere with each other.

The general appearance of the children is to a stranger very striking. The leading character of their countenances is a mixed look of openness, confidence and intelligence, such as is scarcely to be met with among children in their situation. Their animal spirits are always excellent. Their manners and deportment towards their teachers and towards strangers, are fearless and unrestrained, yet neither forward, nor disrespectful. Their general health is so good, that the surgeon attached to the village, who is in the habit of examining the day scholars periodically, states, as the result of an examination, which took place a few weeks since; that, out of 300 children, only three had some slight complaint; and that all the others were in perfect health. The individual literary acquirements of the greater proportion of the older classes, are such as perhaps no body of children of the same age, in any situation, have had an opportunity of attaining. The writer of the present article has had frequent opportunities of examining them individually; and he has no hesitation in saying, that their knowledge on some of the subjects, which have been mentioned, as forming part of their instruction, is superior to his own.

A sufficient degree of friendly emulation is excited amongst them, without any artificial stimulus; but it is an emulation, which induces them to prefer *going forward with their companions*, to *leaving them behind.* Their own improvement is not their only source of enjoyment. That of their companions they appear to witness with pleasure, unmixed with any envious feeling whatever; and to be eager to afford them any assistance they may require. Some of them have voluntarily undertaken, when any of their companions were necessarily absent during some interesting lecture, to give them all the particulars they should be able to recollect of it, as soon as they returned home.

Although there have always been schools at New Lanark, and although the building

F

which is at present employed as a school,
has been open for eight years, yet several
material parts of the system have been in
operation scarcely two years—so that their
ultimate effects cannot yet be fully ascer-
tained. As far as these have yet appeared,
however, they have been most satisfactory.
It has always been found, that those children,
who made the greatest proficiency in their
various studies and acquirements, proved
subsequently, the best, the most industrious
and most intelligent assistants, both as work-
people and domestics.

There are persons, who will admit the
general consistency and excellency of such
a system of education, but who will, never-
theless, object to it, as totally unadapted to
the lower or working classes.

*That true knowledge uniformly conduces
to happiness* is a fact, which, though it was
denied in the dark ages of the world, is very
generally admitted at the present day.

The acquisition of true knowledge, there-

fore, must increase the happiness of those
who acquire it. And if the lower classes
have fewer outward sources of enjoyment,
than their more wealthy neighbours, then
does it become the more necessary and just,
that they should be furnished with means of
intellectual gratification.

We admit, that the lower classes cannot
receive such an education, and yet remain
in their present ignorant and degraded state.
We admit, that it will make them intelligent
and excellent characters. That, when they
are placed in a situation which is really improper, it will necessarily make them de-
sirous of changing and improving it. We
admit, that the real distance between the
lowest and the highest ranks will be de-
creased. That the ultimate result will be
such an improvement of habits, dispositions
and general character in those in subordinate
situations, as will induce us to regard them
in the light of assistants rather than of dependants. We admit, that its general introduction will gradually render all ranks much
more liberal, better informed, more accom-
plished, and more virtuous than the inhabi-

tants of Great Britain are at this moment.
And that, in short, its direct tendency will
be, to enlighten the world, to raise all
classes without lowering any one, and to
re-form mankind from the least even to the
greatest.

But we misconceive its tendency, and
mistake its effects, if we imagine that real,
solid intellectual improvement, will ever induce the lower classes to envy the situation,
or covet the possessions of the wealthy. Or
that it will ever raise any of them above a
proper employment, or render them dissatisfied with any state of things, that is
really beneficial to themselves or useful to
society. Or that it will create seditious
principles, or excite revolutionary ideas in
their minds. Or, in short, if we suppose
that true knowledge will ever conduce to
misery. We are in error if we conceive,
that it is more pleasant to be surrounded
by servile dependants, than by enlightened
assistants—or, if we believe, that even the
selfish interests of the higher ranks can be
promoted by increasing the distance, and
thus widening the breach between them and

another class of their fellow-creatures—or that the sufferings and degradation of the one class can, in any way, increase the actual enjoyment of the other.

Indeed, the idea, that such a notion is deliberately entertained by the higher classes, presupposes in them a want of feeling, inconsistent alike with every superior sentiment, and with their own real or permanent happiness.

APPENDIX.

APPENDIX.

THE following brief " Introduction to the Arts and Sciences," is presented to the public merely to explain what sort of outline it is here recommended to give to children, before entering into further details. It was drawn up for the New Lanark Schools, and has been communicated to the elder classes. The teachers are directed to illustrate each idea by any anecdote or interesting particular, which may occur to them, or by drawings or models; and to encourage the children, after hearing a short portion of it, to repeat and explain that portion in familiar language. This they are generally able to do with considerable facility.

A manuscript of this " Introduction" has been transcribed by some of the elder scholars, in order at once to impress it on their minds, and to improve their style of hand-writing.

THE EARTH

On which we live, is a very large ball. It is nearly round, in the shape of a globe. The hills and
mountains on its surface, even the highest and
largest of them, which are six or seven times higher than any mountain in Great Britain, do not prevent the earth's being round, any more than the
roughness on the skin of an orange prevents the
orange being round; for they are not so large
compared to the whole earth, as the small raised
parts, which make the orange skin rough compared
to the orange. And, therefore, if we were going
to represent the earth by a globe as large as an
orange, we should not make the mountains so large
as these small inequalities on the skin of the orange.

The earth does not seem to us round, but flat,
because we can only see a very, very small part of
the outside of the earth at once; and a small part
of the outside of a large ball is so very like a flat
surface, that we cannot easily distinguish it from
one. But we know that the earth *is* round, because
people, by travelling for two or three years, in the
same direction, came at last to the place they set
out from. These people travelled round the world.

We do not know whether the earth is solid or not; because we have never seen the inside, except a very short way under the surface.

It is always turning round with us. Yet we do not feel it moving, because every thing we see moves along with us. In the same way, that if a ship sails on a smooth sea, and we are in one of the rooms in the inside of the ship, we cannot tell whether the ship is moving or not; for it does not seem to us to move at all.

The earth is warmed by a much larger globe than itself, called the sun. The sun is a very great way from the earth. If it were too near, every thing would be burnt up. If the sun did not give us heat, nothing could grow or live.

A candle, or any light, can only shine on one half of a globe at a time; the other half is dark. In the same way, the sun can only shine on one half of the earth at once, while the other half, on which it cannot shine, must be dark. This is the reason why it is sometimes day, and sometimes night. The part of the earth we are on, is turned to the sun in the daytime, and turned away from it at night.

You will be told afterwards, why the days are sometimes longer, and sometimes shorter; and why it is hot in summer, and cold in winter.

If you were going to draw a picture of a ball,

you could only draw one half of it at once. Then you would require to turn it round, and draw the other half. That is the reason why the whole earth is drawn on two hemispheres. As you cannot draw it round on paper, it seems flat, but each hemisphere should in fact be a half ball. Every other map, although all maps are drawn flat, represents a part of the outside of the large ball we live on, so that, to be quite correct, it should be raised from the paper.

The world, or any part of the world, can be drawn on a very large map, or on a very small one, in the same way that you can draw the same house on a large piece of paper, and make it large, or on a small piece, and make it small. This is called drawing on a *large scale*, or on a *small scale*.

Part of the outside of the earth is covered with water. The part that is not covered with water is called land, and is not quite half as large as the other.

The whole of the outside of the earth is, therefore, either land or water.

The whole of the earth is surrounded by air.

EVERY thing that is in, or on the earth, is called a *substance.* Each of these substances is supposed to consist of very small particles, much too small to be seen.

All these substances remain on, or in the earth, and the different parts of each of them keep together;—because all substances are drawn towards each other, we do not know how or why.

The larger a substance is, the more it draws another to it; because it has more particles than a smaller body, and each of these particles draws a little. This is the reason why the earth draws every substance to itself; or, in other words, why substances *fall* if we let them ; and why they *press* with what is called their *weight,* upon any thing that supports them.

When any body falls, it draws the earth a *very* little upwards, in the same way that the earth draws it downwards. But all bodies are so small compared to the earth, and the earth is so large, compared to them, that we do not see the earth fall to them, or move towards them, and they fall to it.

The different substances on the earth would fall towards each other if they were larger than the earth ; but we never see them do so, because none of them are nearly so large as the earth ; and, therefore, although they *are* drawn to each other, yet the earth draws them towards itself so much more forcibly, that they are held down to the earth, and cannot fall towards each other.

This is the reason that it requires an effort to raise one of our arms or legs, and that it falls again if we let it.

This is the reason, too, why we never fall off the earth when it is turning round; for (because the earth draws us strongly towards itself,) we always remain standing, or sitting, or lying on it. *We call that which is* IN *the earth,* BELOW *us ; and we say, that that which surrounds the earth,* (for instance, the clouds,) *is* ABOVE *us. Therefore,* however the earth turns, we always stand or sit with our feet downwards, and our heads upwards; that is, with our feet turned towards the earth, and our heads away from it.

If a larger substance than the earth were to come near the earth, it would draw the earth to it; that is, the earth, and every thing that is upon the earth, would fall to it; but although there *are* many larger substances than the earth, which you will be told about afterwards, they are not near enough to draw the earth to them.

For, the *nearer* substances are to each other, the more strongly they are drawn together. This is the reason why the small particles of every thing or sub-stance remain together, and why it requires force to separate, cut, or divide any thing.

This inclination of substances to fall towards each other, is called *attraction ;* and when they are drawn together, we say they attract each other.

If substances did not attract each other, any power, that could set them, even in the least degree in motion, (for instance, the wind,) would blow every thing to pieces ; and the whole world would be separated into small particles in a very short time.

Whenever the force of the wind on a substance is stronger than the attraction *of the earth* to that substance, then the substance is lifted into the air; and whenever the attraction becomes stronger than the force of the wind, it falls again.

Whenever the force of the wind on the particles of a substance is stronger than the attraction of these particles *to each other,* then that substance is blown to pieces.

Whenever the attraction of the particles of a body or substance *to the earth* is stronger than their attraction *to each other,* then that body falls to pieces; that is, each of the separate particles the body is made of falls to the earth, *as soon as the* SIZE *of the earth makes the attraction greater, than the* CLOSE- NESS *of these small particles to each other, makes it.* For the force of the attraction always depends on the *closeness* of the bodies, and on their *size.*

Almost all bodies, which we see, are made of two or more substances, and are then called *compound* bodies. The substances these compound bodies are made of, are called *elements,* or *simple bodies.* We very seldom find simple bodies; that is, we very seldom find bodies made of one substance only.

Although there are so *very* many compound bodies, yet there are very few different kinds of simple bodies, but the different ways in which these bodies come together, make the different objects we see; in the same way that, although there are so few letters in the alphabet, you can make so very many words by putting them together.

We can decompose all compound bodies; that is, we can find out the simple bodies they are made of, but we cannot always put the simple bodies together again, so as to form the compounds we decomposed; for instance, we can decompose flesh or bones, and get the simple substances they are made of; but after we have got these, we cannot make flesh and bones of them again.

Every substance belongs to one of three great divisions called Kingdoms, viz.—

The Animal Kingdom ;

The Vegetable Kingdom ; and

The Mineral Kingdom.

Now, I will tell you how you can generally find out to which kingdom any thing belongs.

ANIMALS change, live, move of themselves, and (most of them, if not all,) think.

VEGETABLES change, live, (cannot move of themselves, and are not supposed to think.)

MINERALS change, (do not live, therefore cannot die or fade, cannot, any more than vegetables, move of themselves, or think.)*

Therefore, animals, vegetables, and minerals, or all substances—change; animals and vegetables change and live; animals change, live, move of themselves, and think.

I.—HOW ANIMALS, VEGETABLES, AND MINERALS,

CHANGE.

ALL substances are continually changing, either slowly, or quickly; sometimes increasing; sometimes decreasing; sometimes with little or no change that we can perceive; sometimes by means of an instant and complete change. When animals or vegetables change, so as to increase in size, we say they *grow*.

When an *animal* is born, it is smaller than it will be after it has lived some time. It continues to increase in size, or to grow; sometimes only for some

---

* These divisions and definitions are given, not because they were considered the most critically correct that could be adopted, but because they were thought to be simple, and easy of application.

hours; sometimes for many years, till it has attained its full size. Still, however, the different particles of the animal continue moving about, and becoming altered; and the whole body and appearance becomes changed, but slowly. Animals grow so slowly that we cannot see them growing; but we see after some time, that they have become larger, and that their appearance has become altered.

Vegetables begin to grow from a seed, or from a root, when this seed or root is put into the earth, or sometimes when it is merely put into water. Some parts of vegetables grow upwards; those are the parts we see; some downwards into the earth, and these are called roots. Vegetables grow in general more quickly than animals, but still they scarcely ever grow so quickly, that we can see them growing.—Most vegetables grow during the hot months of the year; and cease to grow, and even lose part of their growth, in winter. The particles a vegetable is made of, move about in it, and become gradually altered, as well as those of an animal. Some vegetables grow much larger than any animals.

Minerals change, as well as animals and vegetables, but in a very different manner to these, and *very* much slower, often without seeming to change at all. Some of them, however, become many thousand times larger than any animal or vegetable.

The whole body of the earth, as far as we know, is composed of minerals, which have been changing for a very long time.

There are a very great many more mineral substances in the earth than animal or vegetable substances; for animal and vegetable substances grow merely on the surface of the earth, whereas, the earth itself is probably made of mineral substances.

II.—HOW ANIMALS AND VEGETABLES LIVE.

You have just been told, that animals, vegetables, and minerals, are continually changing,—sometimes growing larger, sometimes becoming less; but you know, that animals and vegetables grow quite in a different way from minerals. First of all, they grow quicker; then, animals cannot grow unless they are fed, nor vegetables unless they are planted. Then again, animals and vegetables grow larger for a certain time; then they continue nearly the same size; then they become less and less vigorous, till at last they always change completely, and become what we call *dead*. The animal does not move about then, nor take food, as it used to do; the vegetable does not grow in the warm months, and lose its growth in the cold ones, as it used to do. It falls to the ground; and the roots and branches of the

G 2

dead vegetable, and the body of the dead animal, gradually fall to pieces, and mix with the minerals and vegetables around them, and change along with them.

Now, this way in which animals and vegetables change till they die, is called *living ;* and the sudden change they all undergo, when they no longer continue this mode of existence, is called *death*. Minerals do not grow in this way for a time, and then change suddenly ; therefore, minerals do not live or die.

Animals cannot live without eating food, which is either an animal, vegetable, or mineral substance, chiefly a vegetable one; nor without drawing in and breathing out the air with which the. earth is surrounded. If they are without food or air, for a short time, almost all animals will die. This food, and this air, must be proper for the animal, or he cannot live either. Some animals eat one kind of food, and some another. Each different species of animals requires different kinds of food to keep it alive. Some kinds of air, too, would kill an animal, if he were to breathe them : these are sometimes found a little below the surface of the earth. But the air which surrounds the earth is, almost everywhere, fit for breathing; only it is better in one place than another.

Part of the food an animal eats, mixes with the

particles of the body of the animal; and the air the animal breathes takes away some of these particles. These particles are thus continually in motion, so as gradually to change the animal. Most animals have blood, which is red in some, and white in others. It moves about in the body of the animal as long as it lives. If a severe blow or stab prevent these things from going on, the animal is killed.

Some animals do not live for one day; others live for about 200 years. We do not know what is the longest time some animals may live.

Vegetables cannot live, any more than animals, without food, nor without air. Their roots receive nourishment from the ground, or from water, and this nourishment is circulated all over the vegetable. The other parts of the vegetable, particularly the leaves, are acted upon by the air which surrounds it, so that circulation is continually going on throughout the vegetable. Some vegetables require one kind of ground, and some another. Some vegetables live only one summer, and these are called *annuals;* some live longer probably than any animals; some are said to have lived about 1000 years.

If a vegetable be cut in two, that part which remains in the ground generally continues to live, and the other part dies.

Some animals and vegetables can only live in warm countries, and some few only in cold ones.

III.—HOW ANIMALS *MOVE* AND *THINK*.

Some animals move on land, and some in water. Most land animals move about by means of feet, which they put forwards and backwards as they please. A few land animals move without feet, by drawing their bodies together, and then stretching them out again. Some land animals can move about in the air, without touching the land, by means of wings, with which they continue to strike the air, as long as they wish to move about. Water animals move about in the water, by means of fins, which are grisly substances, which they can move at pleasure, so as to answer the purpose of our feet. Only one kind of water animal that we know, can move about in the air, and it can only do so for a short time.

Most animals have five senses; viz. the senses of seeing, hearing, feeling, smelling, tasting. Every thing that surrcunds them makes an impression on the senses, perhaps somewhat in the same way that we can make an impression on any thing, for instance by striking or pressing it. If we strike or press any thing it receives the stroke or pressure; and if any thing comes before our eyes, our eyes receive the image or impression of that thing. If they did not, we could not see what it was like;—and the same with the rest of their senses.

We certainly do not know *how* our senses get these impressions, but we know that they *do* get them; for we see things with our eyes, hear with our ears, feel with our fingers and other parts of our bodies, smell with our noses, and taste with our mouths. If we could not see, hear, smell, taste or feel, we could know nothing of what is about us; so that every thing we know, we know by our senses. We could not think at all if we knew nothing, and we always think according to what we know, or according to these impressions. Therefore these impressions give us thoughts, and after we have thought, then we move about or act. So that you see the impressions which we receive by our senses, cause us to move about or act.

Now Vegetables have not these senses. They do not see, hear, feel, smell or taste. Therefore they can neither think, nor move about, nor act.

———

Now I will tell you what are the different kinds of knowledge, which have been obtained by the senses of different men.

All knowledge belongs either to an *art* or a *science.*

Whatever tells us of the nature and properties of any substance, is a *science.*

Whatever teaches us how to produce any thing, is an *art.*

The principal sciences are—

Astronomy, Geography, Mathematics, Zoology, Botany and Mineralogy—Chemistry.

The arts are—

Agriculture, Manufactures, Architecture, Drawing, (including Sculpture,) Music, and a few others of less importance.

Almost all these arts depend upon sciences, for it is necessary to know what are the nature and qualities of substances, before we can produce them.

I am now going to tell you what these sciences tell us about, and what these arts teach us.

ASTRONOMY.

There are, as I told you, many other very large bodies besides the earth, some of them much larger than the earth. These bodies are the sun, the moon and the stars. Astronomy teaches us all that is yet known about them; and about their sizes and distances from one another. They are so far from this earth, that we do not know much about them.

GEOGRAPHY

Is the knowledge of the countries that are on the surface of the earth. It tells us what these different countries are like, and how they are divided. It tells us of the manners and customs of the people who live in them, and what animals, vegetables and minerals are found there.

MATHEMATICS

Teaches us how to number and to measure different bodies, and how to tell their proportionate sizes to each other.

ZOOLOGY

Is the natural history of animals; or the knowledge of the formation, appearance, habits, and dispositions of animals.

As men and women are animals, it tells us about them; for instance, about their bodies, about the blood, flesh, bones, sinews, joints, and all the different parts of the body. It explains to us, as far as can yet be explained, how they live, how they move about, how they feel and think, and how they should be treated; but in all these things there is a great deal that has not yet been discovered, and that we cannot understand.

That part of the natural history of men and women, which tells us what men and women did before we were born and since that time, is called *History.* We are not sure that all histories are quite true; because the people who wrote them might have been mistaken, or might have written that, which they knew did not happen. However, when different writers of history, who did not know one another and had not seen what one another wrote, tell us the same thing, it is more likely to be true, than when only one writer tells us so.

It is more difficult to tell whether what we read in history is true or not, than whether what we read about the earth and its productions is true, because we can see the earth, and what is on it, but we cannot see what happened before we were born; nor if it be long since, even see the persons, who were there when any event happened.

That part of Zoology which tells us about men and women, is the most important science in the world, because you will grow to be men and women, and then you will find how very useful it is to know as much as is yet known about yourselves. Now although every thing you will hear about yourselves does really belong to Zoology, yet there is so much of it, and it is so very different from the natural history of other animals, that it is generally found convenient not to include it under Zoology, but to divide it into a number of different sciences, which you will hear of when you are older and better able to understand them.

BOTANY

Is the knowledge of all substances that belong to the vegetable kingdom, therefore of all trees, shrubs, flowers, fruits, and other vegetable productions.

MINERALOGY

Is the knowledge of the substances of which the earth is made.

That part of Mineralogy, which tells us about the interior (or inside) of the earth, and about large mineral masses, is called *Geology*.

We know very little about Geology, because we have never been able to get more than two miles into the earth. Now it is 8000 miles through the earth, so that we must have gone 4000 times farther than two miles to see what was all through the earth.

Now I will tell you what the arts are, that I mentioned to you.

AGRICULTURE.

The greater part of the food we eat is produced from the ground. Agriculture is the art of producing this food. It is by far the most useful and necessary employment in the world, because we could scarcely live without it.

MANUFACTURES.

Every thing we wear and every thing we use, except food, is produced by manufactures. The greater part of these things is made by machines. One machine often does as much work as a great many men and women. New machines are found out almost every day.

Small manufactures are often called trades; for instance the trade of a shoemaker, tailor, &c.

ARCHITECTURE

Is the art of building the houses in which men and women live. A hut is a very small house which was easily built, and which has only one or two rooms. A palace is a very large house, which contains many rooms, and which costs much trouble in building.

DRAWING

Is the art of representing objects, so that a person who sees the drawing may know what the object is like, although he has never seen the object itself. The more like the drawing seems to the object it is meant to represent, the better it is done. Most drawings are made on paper, canvass or ivory. Drawings of persons are called portraits.

Sculpture is the art of representing objects by cutting wood or stone like them.

MUSIC

Is the art of producing pleasant sounds by means of the voice, or of different instruments. The knowledge of the rules required to compose music is called Thorough Bass.

MOST of these sciences might be included under CHEMISTRY; and even many of the arts depend upon it; for Chemistry is, in fact—

10

The knowledge of the properties of all sub·
stances, and of the manner in which all simple
substances are combined, and all compound substances decomposed.

Under Chemistry, however, *is generally understood* the knowledge of some of the properties of
such of the simple substances as we have already
discovered, and of a few of their combinations, as
well as the way to make some of these combinations. Even in this contracted signification, Chemistry includes a part of the sciences of Zoology,
Botany and Mineralogy. The substances it tells us
about at present are chiefly minerals; so that it is
the most connected with Mineralogy.

We do not know nearly so much about Chemistry as we may expect to know, when people have
paid more attention to it and tried more experiments.

In order to get an easier knowledge of the
sciences and arts, we learn to read, write, and to
understand languages, the arithmetical signs, and
the musical notes and signs. But these are not
real knowledge. We only learn them, that we
may be able to acquire knowledge by means of
them. All real knowledge is not included in any
of these, but only in the arts and sciences.

Trade or commerce is the system of arrangements, by which the productions of nature and of the arts are at present distributed.

Any new fact in science is called a *discovery*: any new mode of producing, an *invention*.

No science or art is by any means complete. People are learning something new in all of them almost every day. That is; there are discoveries and inventions made almost every day.

GLASGOW:
ANDREW & JOHN M. DUNCAN,
Printers to the University.

THE

ᚠundamental Principles

OF

THE NEW LANARK SYSTEM

EXPOSED,

IN A SERIES OF LETTERS

TO

ROBERT OWEN, Esq.

———

BY W. M'GAVIN.

———

GLASGOW,

PRINTED BY ANDREW YOUNG, 150, TRONGATE.

———

1824.

LETTERS

MR. OWEN'S NEW SYSTEM:

By Wᴹ· M'GAVIN, Glasgow.

No. 1.

INTRODUCTORY LETTER,

TO THE EDITOR OF THE GLASGOW CHRONICLE.

Sir,

I observe in your paper of Tuesday, the 14th instant, a letter by Mr. Owen of New Lanark, in which he announces his intention of publishing, through the medium of the Chronicle, a series of letters, with " a full development of the principles of the New System," which has lately been the subject of much controversy, and which he proposes to place fairly before the public mind.

It is certainly of importance, as he says, that this should be done; not so much on account of the merits of the system itself, as on account of the interest it has excited, and the confidence with which its author continues to maintain it, notwithstanding much opposition and many discouragements which he has experienced, from men of all sects, and of every rank, in the three kingdoms.

Mr. Owen concludes his introductory letter in the following terms, in which he invites a reply, not only to it, but also to those which are to follow:—" To these letters," says he, " I request the calm attention of all classes, sects, and parties. And it becomes the duty of those who shall be able to detect an error in any one of them, to come forward and expose it to the public; more especially, that of the clergy, and the governments of all countries, who, in fact, are intrusted with the formation of the human character, and the direction of human affairs." The first letter of the series, entitled, "*Mr. Owen and the Church of Scotland,*" appeared in your paper of Saturday the 18th instant. I think it contains many errors, which I have the vanity or presumption, (call it what you will,) to believe myself " able to detect;" and therefore, according to Mr. Owen's admission, it becomes *my duty* to come forward and expose them to the public. I am, indeed, neither a clergyman, nor a governor of any country; but perhaps on that account I am a more fit person to enter the lists with Mr. Owen. I am a man of business like himself, having no more interest in any civil or ecclesiastical establishment than he has, but certainly an equal interest in opposing error, maintaining truth, and promoting the welfare of my fellow-creatures. I have besides had the advantage of a business acquaintance with him for more than twenty years, and could speak on the highest terms of his benevolence and zeal, had these always taken a right direction. In short, I have no feeling but that of respect for his personal character, as I believe he has for mine: and therefore I think your readers have reason to expect that the controversy between us will be conducted without any angry feeling on either side.

" If," says Mr. Owen, " that system shall prove to be opposed to nature and to fact, no one can be more anxious than myself, that it should be immediately rejected by every one." This is happily bringing the subject to a plain and simple test; and I shall endeavour to show that both fact and nature are against him, except when by the word *nature*, something bad or degenerate is meant. But, having thus announced my intention, I shall forbear sending you any more, till Mr. Owen shall have finished his series, that I may have his whole system before me at once.

As Mr. Owen comes fairly before the public with his name, it would not be fair to answer him anonymously; and therefore I subscribe myself, Yours, very truly,

W. M'GAVIN.

October 20th, 1823.

TO ROBERT OWEN, Esq.

LETTER FIRST.

Sir,

It was my intention to delay entering on my reply to your letters, till you had finished your series, which you gave reason to expect would extend to only three or four; but as you have already published six, without any intimation that you are near a conclusion, I see no necessity for waiting any longer, especially as your first four letters contain, I presume, the whole theory of your system, or, what you originally proposed, — " a full development of its principles,"—the fifth and sixth relating chiefly to arrangements made with your partners, and your proceedings at New Lanark, which do not contain much matter that calls for animadversion from me. My design is not to find fault with your operations, but to expose the fallacy of certain principles which you inculcate as the foundation of your system, and the evil consequences to which they unavoidably lead.

On entering on the subject, I cannot but express my approbation of a rule which you have prescribed,—that in discussing a subject of so much importance as renovating and saving a world lying in " poverty, sin, and misery," (for by your New System you hope to effect no less) all personalities ought to be laid aside, every inferior consideration kept out of view; and that we should think only of what shall impart the greatest benefit to our species. This is good and wholesome doctrine; but I was a little disappointed to find that you lost sight of it in the very instant of proposing it; for at the beginning of your first letter, (see Glasgow Chronicle of 18th Oct.) you make an attack on " some of the Scottish clergy," then on the " General Assembly of Scotland," and, lastly, on " the Church of Scotland in its official capacity." It is true you do not give the names of persons; but personalities do not consist in that alone: your accusation attaches to every member of the last General Assembly as much as if you had named him; and by implication it must attach to the whole Church of Scotland, at least to her Clergy. You represent them as alarmed at the success of the New System; and attacking both its principles and practice before they were acquainted with either. This is holding them up to their people in a very odious light. If it be true that you have made one community enlightened and happy, and that you are about to impart the same blessing to the whole empire, and then to the whole world, what must those Clergymen be but enemies to the human race, seeing they are alarmed by the success of your exertions, and set themselves to oppose them, before they are acquainted with either the principles or the practice which they oppose? They must indeed, as you seem to insinuate, be actuated by an innate love of darkness, and hatred of light, like a company of bats and owls, who would prevent the rising of the sun if they could. The question at present is not whether your accusation be just or unjust—that is no busi-ness of mine—the Scotish Clergy do not need the aid of my pen: but while you profess to renounce the " spirit of the old world," and to engage in a "*friendly* competition, to discover what is true and beneficial for our common nature," you ought to have avoided such injurious person-alities. You ought at least to allow that the Reverend Gentlemen acted from the honest conviction of their own minds, as you wish to have conceded to you, and not from the mere spirit of opposition to a thing they knew nothing about.

Persons who have not seen the New System in operation may be unacquainted with its practice; but no person who has paid attention to your publications can be ignorant of its principles, at least so far as they are capable of being understood. In your first letter you give a summary of them in twelve distinct propositions, which you lay down as so many axioms, or self-evident truths, though, as we shall see by and by, some of them are mere truisms, and others not so much; and they are preceded by one general proposition, which you lay down as the foundation of the whole. It is in these words:—" Happiness cannot be en-joyed by a few. All must be happy, before one human being can be perfectly so. I doubt indeed whether *any* being can be happy while he is conscious that another exists in misery." You admit the deplorable fact that the world is full of " poverty, sin, and misery;" then you must doubt if there be a happy being in the universe; or that if there be one, he must be ignorant of such a world as ours! Your doctrine is shortly this:—Millions of men are miserable; but no *being* can be happy while he knows of another being who is unhappy: ergo, there is no Supreme Being; or if there be, he is ignorant of the existence of misery, or he is himself unhappy. Here I give you the choice of three things, to one or other of which your fundamental proposition unavoidably leads:—First, there is no God; or, secondly, God does not know that creatures are miserable; or, thirdly, he is unhappy! Choose which you will, you believe an absurdity, to match which I have found nothing even in the abominations of popery. Papists, I know, eat their god hundreds of times in their lives; but he is not a bit the worse for that; they believe him to be perfectly happy notwithstanding; and that he has perfect knowledge of all things. But your god, if you have one, is either ignorant or miserable! He has been so for six thousand years; (for in your first letter you admit this to be the period of the existence of sin and misery) and he must continue so till your system shall prevail over the earth, and over hell too, if you will admit of such a place. Then when you have restored both the living and the dead to perfect happiness, your god will begin to be happy also! But then how can you make either the dead or the living happy, since you have told them of another being, and he the greatest of all, who is unhappy? The thing is impossible, according to your own showing; and therefore misery —hopeless, universal misery must reign to all eternity! This is the fundamental principle of your new system, followed up to its consequences; and truly that must be a goodly fabric that rests on such a foundation. You cannot avoid this deduction from your first principle, otherwise than by denying the existence of a Supreme Being; on which, I confess, you are not very explicit. Once or twice you use the term God; but it is so connected with the word Nature, which indeed you place first in order, that it does not appear which you consider the supreme, or whether they be not equal. I shall proceed, however, on the supposition that you believe in one Supreme Being, unless you shall avow the contrary; and then I shall argue with you on other ground, if I shall find, on reflection, that such an avowal leaves any ground to argue upon.

Do not suppose that I really accuse you of believing in an ignorant or a miserable divinity; for I do not think you capable of such impious absurdity; but as this, or direct atheism, is the unavoidable consequence of your fundamental principle, I hope a simple exposure of its monstrous deformity will induce you to abandon your whole system, and return to sober reason and common sense. I suspect my own feelings have become somewhat obtuse with regard to such matters, else my hand would not have been able to guide my pen to write the horrible consequence of your doctrine, that the Fountain of all knowledge must not know the state of his own world; or that knowing it, the Author of all happiness must himself be unhappy, till *you* shall have rectified the disorders of the universe!

The top-stone of your temple, that is your 12th proposition, is, as a top-stone ought to be, of the same materials, but of a lighter composition than your foundation-stone. It is, " That no *human* being can be truly happy, while he is conscious that another exists in misery." This is not so revolting as your fundamental proposition, which includes all, or " *any* being," but it is liable to the same objection; for what is not inconsistent with the perfect felicity of the Divine Being, is not inconsistent with the happiness of any creature whom he is pleased to make after his own image, and teach to approve what he approves, and to condemn what he condemns. To deny this would be to deny the goodness and power of God; as if he could not make some creatures happy, because others choose to make themselves miserable; for I maintain that the misery of creatures is entirely of themselves; and that God never made any creature miserable, who had not made himself so. Thus, your system, in its most modified form, represents the Creator as dependent on creatures who choose to be sinful, and of course miserable; insomuch, that while they please to continue in that state, he cannot impart happiness to other creatures whom he shall please to recover from it or preserve from falling into it.

This is another consequence fairly deducible from your doctrine, of which, I believe, you are not aware; and while thus exposing the deformity of your system, agreeably to your own challenge, I beg to be understood throughout, as speaking of your system only, and not of yourself. I am persuaded you do not believe the shocking things which I have here brought to your view; but if they are fair deductions from your first principles, you are responsible for them; and unless you can show that your system is innocent of such consequences, you ought to renounce it without delay.

Your system has, at first view, an appearance of benevolence. It makes the happiness of every individual depend on the happiness of the whole species; and surely that must be a kind and compassionate heart that cannot be happy while conscious that another creature exists in misery. But let us examine this, your first principle, a little more closely, and we shall find that it rests on a mere gratuitous assumption. It has no foundation either in fact or nature. You might say, with equal truth, that

it is impossible for any man to eat while he is conscious
that another man is hungry and destitute: And, no doubt,
if you saw a man without food, or knew of one within
your reach, it would be an amiable and benevolent action
to divide your morsel with him; but suppose there were
starving thousands without your reach, as was the case in
Ireland last year, and there are hundreds, I suspect, nearer
home every year, would you refuse to eat your own dinner
till you were assured that these hundreds or thousands
were equally well provided? Or, suppose you knew a
man in such a diseased state of body that he could not
enjoy, or even take his dinner, would you abstain from
yours till he had recovered his health, and the tone of his
stomach? I am sure that such abstinence, in either case,
would indicate neither benevolence nor wisdom, and I am
persuaded you would be ashamed of such folly.

Now, if the case of happiness be not exactly parallel,
it is so much alike, that it may receive illustration from
what I have here supposed. I admit that it is the duty
of a man to do every thing in his power to promote the
happiness of fellow-creatures; and I admit farther, that
no man can be truly happy while conscious that he is not
doing what he might, and is able to do, for the happiness of others, even though they are beyond the reach of
his personal services. But having done what he could,
there is no reason why he should not be perfectly happy,
either in present enjoyment or future prospect, though
his labours have not been universally successful. To be
unhappy on this account, would be to repine because he
is not omnipotent. Besides, there are some men of such
a diseased state of mind, that they cannot possibly enjoy
happiness. They are under the influence of their evil de-
sires and passions, and refuse to be reclaimed. These
desire happiness to be sure, in their own sense of the
word, that is, the full and uncontrolled gratification of

their lusts. Now, the happiness of such would be the misery of all the world besides; and is it reasonable that some should not enjoy happiness in the way of righteousness, because others prefer the way of wickedness, which is immutably the way of misery?

Your system makes the happiness of every one depend upon the happiness of all; which is precisely the same as making the happiness of all depend upon that of any one; for if so much as one individual shall choose to stand out, and prefer his own vicious gratification to his own real happiness, (and there have always been thousands of such in the world,) then the whole species must yield to him. No one can be happy; the whole race must be miserable, because *one* chooses to be so; how much more, when many thousands make the same choice, as we know well to be the fact in the present age, as history declares to be the fact in the ages that are past! and you can give no security stronger than your bare word, that it shall not be the same in the ages to come.

Now, what you call the old system, at least the only system which I acknowledge as of any authority in this matter, insures the happiness of countless multitudes, without the contingency which hangs like a millstone about the neck of your system. You propose happiness *to none* unless *every one* be willing; the old system insures it to *every one who is willing*, though some *will not*. There is no such thing as making creatures happy against their will. The very coercion would make a beggar miserable at the king's table, and a sinner wretched in heaven. Your system possesses no means of influencing, or operating a change in the mind of a sinner, so that he shall choose the good, and refuse the evil; and supposing but one in the universe to remain unchanged, your system has no room for the happiness of a single individual. Supposing, then, your system to prevail, it would lead the whole human race to endless perdition; and you would have the unenviable distinction of being, what I am sure you do not wish to be, the leader in the march of misery; unless, indeed, a distinguished personage, who has held that office from the beginning, should refuse to resign.

These things have no necessary connection with your rational and practicable measures for improving the condition of the labouring classes. You understand your own business well. You can calculate the result of certain mechanical powers, according to the laws of nature; for I have no objection to this expression, when applied to certain known properties which the Creator has imparted to matter. You did right to improve your knowledge of these things to profitable purposes. Nay, you acquired extensive acquaintance with the character, habits, and domestic economy of many hundreds of labouring men and women, many of whom did not know how to apply their small means to the most profitable ends, or how to make themselves and families so comfortable as their means afforded; and many of them no doubt have to thank you for the lessons you have taught, and the arrangements which you have made, for their comfort. Had you confined your attention to these things, which you understand so well, and communicated the result of your experiments to the proprietors of similar establishments; nay, had you endeavoured to form villages in different parts of the country, where people would be taught industry, economy, and every other art and science that could minister to their personal and family comfort, you would have been entitled to the gratitude of the country at large. And with your means you might have done much good in this way, without impugning the Christian religion, and without committing yourself on metaphysical and theological questions, about which you have no knowledge whatever. By your own account, repeated for the thousandth time, you meant

not to interfere with the religious opinions of any party;
and yet in your letters, which I have before me, you not
only avow principles which are subversive of all religion,
but you make the success of your system to depend on the
universal abandonment of those religious principles which
all sects of Christians hold sacred. Now, when you con-
nect the temporal benefit which you propose to impart to
mankind, with the adoption of a system of error and impiety, subversive of the eternal interests of every one who
embraces it, you forfeit all claim to our gratitude. Nay,
you extort the opposition of every right-minded man in the
community; for " it becomes," as you say, " the duty
of those who shall be able to detect" your errors, " to
come forward and expose them to the public." You will
reply, that I am proceeding according to the " old system," which you have exploded; and that your system
knows nothing about " eternal interests," or any interest
beyond those of the present life. Yes, and this is the
very thing of which I complain. You rob the soul of its
best hopes, and its only true happiness; and you present,
in return, nothing but the picture of a beautiful village,
like a painted cage, in which the silly creatures whom you
shall decoy, shall flutter for a few days, and then fall into
nothing. Your system, like the forbidden fruit, may be
pleasant to the eye; but the taking and eating of it, is
perdition.

Here you will detect me proceeding upon the old system again; for as you acknowledge neither soul nor future
life, so far as appears, you have nothing to do with perdition. I am aware of this, too: but you have no right
to avail yourself of your own peculiar principles, till you
have proved them, or had them admitted. I am entitled
to argue upon generally, if not universally, acknowledged
principles, till they are proved to be erroneous; and the
man who comes to impugn what is established in public

opinion, ought to bring with him demonstrative proof that it is founded in error. I grant, that a principle being established, or generally received, is not a proof of its truth; but it gives it a title to public respect, until sufficient reason shall be brought against it. Here the burden of proof rests with you, and you have adduced nothing yet that deserves the name. Your most sweeping condemnation of things both divine and human, proceeds upon no higher authority than your bare word. So *you* will have it, and so it *must be!* If you say you appeal to reason, you use a mere figure of speech, which is of as much value in my hand as in yours; for you cannot produce the goddess of reason, *in propria persona*, on your side, any more than I can do on mine; and my *nay* will go as far as your *yea*, all the world over.

The fact is, you consider mankind as mere machines, or what you call " passive compounds," possessing no more of an immortal spirit than your great water-wheel; and you think you can regulate their movements as easily as you can do those of your great and small gear. This is another of your fundamental principles, which I shall proceed to examine in my next.—In the mean time, I am, Sir, Yours, &c.

W. M'GAVIN.

17, *Queen-street, 4th Nov.* 1823.

A. YOUNG, PRINTER,
150, Trongate, Glasgow.

LETTERS

MR. OWEN'S NEW SYSTEM:

By Wᴹ· M'GAVIN, Glasgow.

No. 2.

.I REQUEST the reader's attention for a few moments, before he read my Second Letter to Mr. Owen, that I may explain the nature and object of this controversy. I have an apprehension that some of my readers will be disappointed in both the matter and style of what follows. Those of them who did me the honour of following me for four years through a periodical controversial publication, will probably expect to find in these Letters some serious scriptural argument, and illustration of scripture doctrine, such as they were accustomed to find in the pages of " THE PROTESTANT;" but, for a time at least, they must allow me to occupy ground neither so profitable for them, nor so pleasant to myself. The Church of Rome, with all her faults, maintains certain fundamental principles, which, though perverted in the use and application of them, constitute a common ground on which Protestants can stand and dispute with her. But with Mr. Owen I have not an inch of common ground, except his admission of the fact that men are somehow in a sinful and miserable state. But we can agree no farther than the mere admission of the fact; for we differ essentially about both the cause and the remedy. I have presumed upon his readiness to admit the other common ground of the existence of One Supreme Being; but, as he has not explicitly done so, I cannot proceed with much confidence upon it, in the way of arguing directly with himself. To reason with him upon scriptural principles, therefore, would be quite nugatory; and to adduce texts from the Bible against him, would only excite his contempt.

B

I am therefore reduced to the necessity of placing myself hypothetically on his ground, however narrow; that is, of taking the little which he admits, and trying his own principles and arguments by it, tracing them to their consequences, and showing to what absurdity and mischief they would lead. It has generally been understood that an author is sufficiently refuted, when it is shown that his principles lead to absurdity or atheism. In my First Letter to Mr. Owen, I think, it will appear that he is reduced to the choice of one or other of these, unless, indeed, he shall prefer both.

His language, however, is so far from being clear and precise, that it is probable I may have mistaken his meaning in some instances, which shall be cheerfully acknowledged when it is pointed out. In the passage which is the subject of animadversion in the immediately following Letter, his meaning seems to be, that man has no *natural* superiority above the beast; which is corroborated by the whole tenor of his system, in which he treats man merely as a creature of time. I found it impossible to oppose this by serious argument, without going off the little common ground on which we stand; and could only expose the absurdity of the thing in a style which some serious persons will consider bordering on levity.

It is not, however, my intention to confine myself long in such trammels. When I have shown the absurdity of Mr. Owen's leading principles, I shall proceed seriously to expose to his view a system, which really effects all the good which he proposes to do by his, and a great deal more. But I must first prepare the way by showing the folly and inefficacy of his system, and of every other which rejects the Christian Revelation.

TO ROBERT OWEN, Esq.

LETTER SECOND.

SIR,

IN my last letter I followed up the fundamental principle of your New System to its legitimate consequences. I showed that it led either to atheism, or to this horrible consequence, that there is no happiness in the universe, either for the Creator or his creatures. I proceed now to examine your doctrine as laid down systematically in your first letter. It is a curious coincidence, that it contains exactly the same number of articles, as what is called the Apostles' creed, and which correspond with the number of the Apostles themselves,—each, according to the monkish tradition, having composed an article. Your twelve propositions however did not require the labour of so many hands. I believe they are entirely your own, and I shall proceed to examine them in order.

That which I have shown to issue in universal misery, you call the " science" of human happiness, which " science," you say, " has been derived from an attentive examination of the laws of nature, and it is founded solely on those laws."

The first of which is—

" That human nature, like each distinct species of animal nature, is always composed of the same general propensities, faculties and qualities, but that these differ in degree and combination, in every individual of the human race."

This, it seems, is the first law of nature, and as it relates to herself in one of the numerous combinations in which she exists, it surely ought to be very simple and intelligible. I cannot say it is so; but it seems to signify that nature, like a prudent mother, puts all her children on an equal footing; she places herself in her human combination, on a level, or nearly so, with herself in every species of animal combination or composition, so that one has little or no pre-eminence above another. Your language indeed does not explicitly bear this; but as you use no higher standard of comparison than that of the animal creation, it may be fairly inferred, that you consider man as a mere animal. There is a want of precision in your language, which makes it very difficult to know the full extent of your meaning. If it be your meaning that man and beast, so far as nature is concerned, are perfectly equal; and that any difference which may appear to distinguish the former from the latter is entirely the effect of art, of education, or of circumstances;—if, I say, this be your meaning, as I suspect it is, you ought to say so plainly, and not leave it to be inferred from an ambiguous mode of expression, like the Delphic Oracle, which may mean any thing or nothing. You do nature great injustice by making her speak in this way, while propounding her laws, which ought at least to be as intelligible as those of any human lawgiver. On a careful examination of your twelve articles, which comprehend the whole laws of nature, I see nothing by which human nature is preferred to animal nature, except the great variety of degree and combination of propensities, faculties and qualities, which you say exists in every individual of the human race; while you ascribe nothing of the kind to any individual beast; from which I infer that you consider propensities, faculties, and qualities, to exist in the same degree and combination in every individual beast of the same species.

Now, supposing this to be your opinion, you acted unwisely by beginning your experiments with the human race. Such is the infinite variety of degree and combination of propensities, faculties and qualities, in every individual man, that it is impossible you can produce any effect upon more than two or three in your whole life; and your success with any one gives no assurance of success with any other; whereas, if you succeed with one individual brute, you gain his whole species. You ought to try this yet, and let human beings alone, till you have proved the efficacy of your system upon a community of dogs, or foxes, of which there are still some in the Upper Ward of Lanarkshire; and it is but fair that you should have the advantage of beginning with the most sagacious of the brute race. Bring all the laws of nature to bear upon them, which you may easily do, for they have no religious prejudices to surmount; and these form the greatest obstacle to your success with the human race. When you have succeeded in training the inhabitants of the proposed canine settlement to speak, and read, and write, and reason as well as yourself, though I would not call it perfection, I would pronounce it such a degree of improvement, as ought to encourage you to try your system upon the far more incorrigible race of man.

Your forming an establishment of the kind here suggested, would be of great advantage in another way. It would shut the mouths of nine-tenths of the objectors to your system; for human beings are strange compounds, though I cannot, like you, call them *passive* ones. They have an idea that they are somehow superior to the brutes; and they do not like to see themselves or fellow human beings made the subjects of mere experiment, like dead frogs under a galvanic battery. And, in point of fact, the most eminent physiologists have preferred a dog, or cat, or some other creature of the same rank in society, when they wished to ascertain the effect of certain poisons upon the vital powers. Now, I do most earnestly exhort you to do the same; and you may rest assured of being allowed to make your experiments without molestation; for whether human beings hold their superiority by usurpation or not, they have the advantage of possession, which is nine-tenths of the law, and will not readily consent to be brought down to a level with the beasts; though few will object to your raising the beasts to their level if you can.

I have not forgotten that I proposed to shew that according to your system, men are mere machines; but humanity itself would not allow me to see human nature cast down so low, without breaking its fall by a momentary standing upon the brute level, which is a situation of real dignity, in comparison of that occupied by dead matter, however ingeniously formed for mechanical purposes. To this, however, you do bring human nature, in your second article, which is :—

" That each human being comes into the world a *passive compound*, and in some respects unlike every other individual of his species."

A compound, according to Dr. Johnson, is " a mass formed by the union of many ingredients." Passive, according to the same authority, is " receiving impression from some external agent—unresisting—not opposing." This is a correct description of a block of wood, or any other simple mass of matter; but a passive compound is like a pudding stone, or rather a plumb-pudding, which consists of many ingredients in a united mass; but as dead and inactive as a block. In this state, you believe man comes into the world; and you propose to hew and mould him to reason and happiness, just as you form any other block into an instrument or vessel fit for use; but if he should fall into bad hands, he will be formed into an instrument of mischief, as a ploughshare and a dagger are formed of the same metal. Now, I admit that man is so far passive, that he is susceptible of impressions from external agents, to a blow on the head for instance; but I maintain that he is active too, and that in the first moment of his visible existence, for the truth of which I shall use no argument, but merely appeal to all the mothers and nurses in the world.

But I suppose you mean his passiveness to relate to the state of his mind and not of his body. There is, however, no more truth in the one opinion than in the other, though I cannot prove his mental activity by such a direct appeal to the evidence of sense. This is a matter of individual consciousness, of which every man may judge for himself; and if any man shall tell me that he is not conscious of the activity of his own mind, and of the voluntariness of his actions, I shall consent that you make him a spoke to one of your wheels. This, however, will come more properly in my way when I come to your doctrine of non-accountability.

I am, SIR, &c.

W. M‘GAVIN.

17, *Queen-street, 7th Nov.* 1823.

TO ROBERT OWEN, Esq.

LETTER THIRD.

SIR,

IN order to avoid the error of writing too long a letter, as my first one was, for the convenience of newspaper readers, I concluded my second with only a passing allusion to what is implied in your second proposition, about man coming into the world a " passive compound." This expression is so general, that it is not easy to say precisely what you mean by it. But taking the words in their common acceptation, they seem to imply such a total privation of activity, will and affection, as places the human

race considerably below the rank of even the beasts of
the field; for we all know that they are not without activity;
and not without certain powers of will and affection, by
which they love and choose some things, and dislike and
reject others.

It is but fair, however, that you should be heard in explanation of your own doctrine; and though the words of
your second proposition imply what is above, and in my last
letter, deduced from them, I admit that in some part of
your letters, and in your other writings, you proceed upon
the supposition that man has some active powers; but that
he is so completely passive in the use of them, that his actions are not properly his, but those of some external
agent who acts upon him. From which it follows that he
is not accountable for either his deeds or misdeeds. Let
his conduct be ever so good, he is not entitled to reward;
and let his crimes be ever so great, he is not justly liable to
punishment. That this is your doctrine, at least with regard
to children and youth, appears from your " Second Address, delivered at the City of London Tavern, on Thursday,
August 21st, 1817," as quoted by your Reviewer in the
Christian Instructor for March last. " After stating somewhat allegorically," says the Reviewer, " that charity,
demonstrable truth, and sincerity, are to preside as the active agents, over the whole dominion of the New State of
Society," you thus proceed :—

" They decreed it to be just, *that as Nature was always
passive before birth, in infancy, childhood and youth, and
was made beneficially or injuriously active by the treatment
she had previously experienced,* THAT NATURE COULD DO
NO WRONG; *and therefore could never become a proper subject for punishment—that the cause of all her errors proceeded from the powers that acted upon her in her passive state—
and that if they were consistent and proper,* NATURE
WOULD BECOME ACTIVELY GOOD, *and in consequence* UNI-

VERSALLY BELOVED; *but if they were irrational and impro-*
per, NATURE WOULD BECOME DISGUSTING AND WICKED,
and in consequence, DISLIKED AND HATED BY ALL."

By nature in this passage, you mean men and women, or
rather boys and girls, as you do not make their passiveness
to extend beyond the period of youth, but during that period
you make them so completely passive and non-accounta-
ble for their actions, that, let them do what they will, they
can never become proper subjects for punishment. Now
this is representing young persons no better than blocks, or
rather a great deal worse. It can be shown that blocks are
active in their own way most innocently and beneficially ;
for in every particle of matter, and of course in every block,
there is an active power, by which it inclines to draw all
things to itself, which however, is regulated by the same
power in every other block, so nicely balanced, that no evil
ever accrued from it. No external agent in the world is
able to impart to a block more of this attractive power than
justly belongs to it ; and in point of fact no individual of
that species was ever convicted of appropriating what was
not his own. Now, if the active power of man were always
as passively, and of course harmlessly employed, he would
not deserve punishment. But you know, that this is not
the case. You know that there has been a fearful increase
of crime, especially of theft and robbery, of late years, among
the young ; and no man can tell how much the principles
inculcated by you may have contributed to it. Upon your
principles, stealing is no crime in a young thief. It is only
the active power inherent in a passive compound, attracting
something to itself, according to impressions made upon it
by some external agent; and if there be any thing wrong
in the matter, the fault is not that of the thief, but of the
agent, who is an active being called CIRCUMSTANCES ; who,
so far as appears, is a creature of your own imagination.

It is impossible to estimate the mischief which this doctrine of yours is calculated to produce upon the whole mass of the community, especially the young, thoughtless and ignorant. You certainly do not intend to train up the rising generation to theft and every other crime ; but if you did intend it, you could not pursue means more effectual. You have not only removed the fear of punishment in another state of existence, but you teach, as plainly as you can, that it is unjust to punish men, at least young men, in the present life, whatever their crimes may be. You have spent many years of your life, and thousands of pounds of your money, in giving publicity to your principles, in making them accessible to persons of all ages and ranks of society; and you not only teach the young that they ought not to be punished though they steal, but you also inculcate the doctrine, that judges and magistrates, who put in force the laws against delinquents, are unjust and cruel, thus exciting disaffection and sedition against all existing authority.

In your new View of Society you tell us that you happened, on a particular occasion, to be in Newgate, where you saw a young man, 16 years of age, subjected to the punishment of double irons, for some atrocious offence, when instead of blaming the young man for his crime you lay all the blame on the Home Secretary of State, then Lord Sidmouth, in the following words, which are among the most plain and intelligible of all your writings, except that in the first sentence we might suppose you mean the King, rather than his chief Secretary:—

" The chief civil magistrate of the country in such a case, is far more guilty than the boy ; and, in strict justice, if a system of coercion and punishment be rational and necessary, he (THE CHIEF MAGISTRATE !) ought rather to be doubly ironed, in place of the boy. The Secretary of State for the home department, has long had the power, and ought to have used it, to give that and every other boy in the empire better habits, and to place them under circumstances, that would train them to become moral." See the passage at length, with most pertinent animadversion, in the Christian Instructor for March last, to which, so far as I know, you never made any reply.

Thus you labour not only to rob men of all their hopes of happiness in a world to come, but you do every thing in your power to produce anarchy and insubordination in the present world. I do not say this is your intention, but such, undoubtedly, is the consequence of principles which you inculcate, with all possible zeal and perseverance; and therefore, with a feeling of perfect good will for yourself, I maintain that all good subjects, and right minded men, of every description, ought to unite to put down, by argument, by writing and printing, and circulating tracts as extensively as you have done, your visionary and insane projects. So far from connecting this with hostility to your person, I am persuaded, it is the best way that the public can express their friendship and regard for you; for a gentleman of your large property and extensive connections, would be among the first victims of that new system of things, which, with the most blinded infatuation, you are determined to force upon the world. You hint, in some of your tracts, that it would tend much to improve our health and morals, if we would all go naked, or as nearly so as possible. There would then be little more occasion for spinning or weaving; and though the consequence of this would be the ruin of your great establishment, this would be found a small matter in comparison of the wreck and destruction that would attend the general prevalence of your principles, which teach that the crime of subjects ought to be punished in the persons of their governors.

I know you will evade these conclusions by ascribing them all to my ignorance. I am arguing, you will tell me, upon the principles of *old society;* but that in the *new state* which you are about to introduce, none of the evils which

I apprehend can take place. I know *you say so;* and this is all that the world knows of the matter. I bring the question to your own test, that of nature and fact. It is a fact that human nature is, and has been, according to all history, prone to evil, notwithstanding the restraints of law; and that where such restraints do not exist, or have been removed, it is a thousand times worse, of which you and I are old enough to recollect an example in the case of the French Revolution. I know you have not the means of regenerating a single individual; for the evil lies too deep in human nature to be removed, or even reached by such means as yours; and I defy you to produce an individual whose character has been materially improved by your system. I shall admit there are many worthy individuals in New Lanark. I shall even for argument's sake admit, that the state of morals is equal to that of any other village in the kingdom. This, however, is not owing to your principles, but in spite of them. Good principles were inculcated there by your predecessor, and have been since by some of your own servants; nay, your very inconsistency, in having so long allowed the Bible to be read in your schools, has been of immense benefit. To these causes all the good morals of the people are to be ascribed, and not to your new views and principles.

I am, Sir, yours, &c.

W. M'GAVIN.

12th November, 1823.

A. YOUNG, PRINTER,
150, Trongate, Glasgow.

LETTERS

MR. OWEN'S NEW SYSTEM:

By Wᴹ· M'GAVIN, Glasgow.

No. 3.

TO ROBERT OWEN, Esq.

LETTER FOURTH.

Sir,

THE question of human accountability is
entitled to a much more serious discussion, than I have yet
ventured upon in my controversy with you. But it is impossible to argue seriously upon it, without taking for
granted some things which you do not explicitly grant;
such as the existence of One Supreme Being, to whom we
owe our existence, on whom we constantly depend, and to
whom our ultimate account must be given. I have proceeded upon the presumption of your believing in the existence of such a being; but I am doubtful, if you will admit of your dependence upon him; and I am certain that,
unless you have changed your mind, you will not admit of
being accountable to him; for this is inconsistent with one
of your first principles, that we are " passive compounds;"
and not entitled to reward, or justly subject to punishment
for our actions.

I shall not therefore enter more deeply into the subject,
until I acquire more light from your writings, as to what
you really believe and teach upon it. But I shall here
mention the notorious fact, that there is in the minds of
men, a very general, I may say, universal conviction, that

C

they are accountable to a Superior Being. You will find this among the rudest savages in the world; and as you cannot mention a tribe or family in the earth who have not some notion of a God, so you cannot mention one, who have not the corresponding notion of their being accountable to him for their actions. Hence the universality of sacrifice and other rites intended to propitiate the Superior Being. Now this is fact, and nature too, if you will; and I call upon you to account for it upon your principles. If men have been universally deceived upon this subject, you can surely tell us how you came to know the truth of the matter; and by what power you were destined to enlighten the world.

As for the accountability of creatures to one another, as of subjects to Magistrates, it is well for you and me that the civil institutions which you condemn, make persons accountable, whether they will or not. It may be admitted that our penal code is too sanguinary, and that the punishment of the guilty has very seldom the effect which good men desire; but if there was no such thing as punishing men for their crimes, this world, and even this kingdom, enlightened as it is, would soon become too hot for either of us to live in. I appeal again to nature and fact; and I call upon you to name the people or nation, that ever existed in comfort for a single day, where persons guilty of crimes were not subject to punishment. If you can by your system banish crime, I shall consent that punishment shall cease; but this is no more than the Old System will do as cheerfully as yours. The folly of your plan is to abolish punishment first, and leave crime to follow at its own leisure; and if there be any truth in nature and fact, you may rest assured it will be in no haste.

I proceed now to your third general proposition, which is :—

" That of himself, he (i. e. man, or each human being)

knows not how or why he came into the world, or any thing of the Power which gave him existence."

This, I think, is incontrovertibly true. This, and some other things about himself, man *of himself* does not know. I could tell you how he comes to know it notwithstanding. But how can you tell it, or how do you know it, upon your principles? You, as an individual of the human race, know nothing of the matter *of yourself.* Then how did you come to know it at all? or do you indeed know it? If you do not, you are a very unfit person to be a teacher of others; but if you do know it, some one must have told you, for according to your own doctrine you know it not of yourself. Now, who was *your* teacher? From whom did you receive your perfect knowledge of how and why human beings came into the world, and of the power which gave them existence? Have you had a revelation from the invisible world in your private ear? If so, you ought to tell us all about it, and you can doubtless perform some miracle, or give us some sort of evidence that you have received such knowledge of man, as man does not know of himself. You must show your credentials before you can expect to be received as a prophet.

It is related of Lord Herbert, I think, that when he had finished a book against Divine Revelation, he took the manuscript in his hand, and prayed to the Deity, that if he was mistaken, he might be convinced of his error; and that if he was right, he might receive some Divine intimation of it, to confirm his infidelity. It happened at that very moment, that a cloud passed away, and the sun shone upon the manuscript; and he who laboured to disprove *all* Divine Revelation, took this as a Revelation from Heaven to himself! In short, there are no such enthusiasts in the world as the infidel ones; and I am afraid I must class you among them, unless you can give a more rational account of the manner in which you, who reject the Christian

Revelation, came to receive one of your own, teaching you to know what man of himself does not know.

If you shall confess, as I suppose you will, that you never had any Divine Revelation, then you are as ignorant as other men; and as you do not believe that a Divine communication to any other was ever made, your doctrine comes to this, that we know nothing at all of how or why we came into the world, or of the Power that gave us existence. Here again your system lands us in heartless atheism, unless you shall commence prophet, like Mahomet, and tell us what Revelations you have had, especially how you came to know that about God and man, which man of himself does not know.

Your fourth proposition is:—

" That human beings have no controul whatever, in creating the difference which constitutes individual character at birth."

This is such a ridiculous truism, that it is impossible to make serious argument to bear upon it. The fifth is little better :—

" That without any choice of their own they come into the world either in Europe, Asia, Africa, or America; and in some particular country and district of that country within these divisions."

All this is admitted; and what then?

" 6th, That the circumstances existing in the class, sect, district, and country, in which the human being is born and lives, essentially contribute to give him his language, manners, habits, dispositions, ideas, sentiments, religion, feelings, and conduct."

Here there is something that may be admitted, and much that may be disputed. You, for instance, were born in Wales; and if the place of birth *essentially* contributes to give men their religion along with the other things enumerated, how comes it that your religion is so different from that of other persons who were born in the same country? If you say, when you began to think for yourself, you saw cause to renounce the errors in which you had been educated, and to adopt a more rational system, you say no more than what any Christian who was born in Turkey may say; and your whole proposition falls to the ground as without meaning, or with so little meaning as not to deserve a formal admission of its truth, or refutation of its error.

As the remaining articles of your code of Nature, would perhaps suffer in being separated, I shall give them here entire and in order:—

" 7th, That the impressions necessarily made by these circumstances on the original compound of propensities, faculties, and qualities, given to each individual at birth, do, in fact, and without a single exception, form the whole character of every human being through every moment of his existence.

" 8th, That the will of every human being is itself solely formed by the combined influence of all those causes.

" 9th, That even the will of man, although thus formed, has no controul over his belief or opinions. He must think and believe, in the first place, according to the impressions which external circumstances have made on his individual nature; and afterwards he must continue to think and believe, or his thoughts and belief must change, in obedience to subsequent impressions, or according to the reflections which he shall be enabled to make, by comparing together the previous impression which external circumstances had made on his mental faculties.

" 10th, That the affections and feelings do not depend upon the will of man, but are necessarily produced by the impressions made by external objects on the particular constitution of each individual: and conduct is the combined result of feelings and opinions.

" 11th, That each human being is formed with a desire for happiness; and that he retains that desire through life.

" 12th, That no human being can be truly happy, while he is conscious that another exists in misery."

I admit the truth of the 11th; I disposed of the 12th in my first letter; and as for the others, from the 7th to the 10th, inclusive, I am quite unable to extract a single idea from them; I have read them in the usual way, I cannot tell how often; and I have even tried to read them backwards, thus " opinions and feelings of result combined," as at the end of the 10th, but I can make no more sense of them this way than the other. In short, I have read nothing so incomprehensible, since I had my brain puzzled with the following sentence in Don Quixote:—" The reason of the unreasonableness of your reason so confounds my reason that I have reason to expostulate with your reason;" or the following rhymes, which have been lying so long in a corner of my memory, that I am not sure where I found them; I think they are called " A clear and satisfactory explanation of the doctrine of liberty and necessity," which I suspect has often puzzled you, as it has done others:—

> " I grant that whatsoever may,
> That also can; for can doth may obey:
> But he that may and can is more than man:
> For can may may, but may can never can."

This is not quite incomprehensible, though I shall not pretend to put it into intelligible words.

Now, I candidly confess that I cannot answer these four propositions of yours, because I cannot understand them. You are fairly entitled to all the advantage that this admission will give you. But as your professed object is the improvement of the human race, you ought to write in language level to human capacity. In your first four letters there is much that I cannot comprehend; but in my next I shall proceed to animadvert on such passages as are intelligible and erroneous.—Meantime, I am, &c.

18th November, 1823.

W. M'GAVIN.

TO ROBERT OWEN, Esq.

LETTER FIFTH.

SIR,

I HAVE received several letters from persons who profess to approve your principles and plans upon the whole, though some of them do not go all your length. One is extremely angry, which shows that he has not learned the best part of your discipline, that is, to command his temper. Another suggests that your *practical arrangements* may be beneficially adopted independently of your speculative opinions; and I think I admitted as much in my first letter, in which I disavowed all interference with your practical and useful operations, and only engaged, in obedience to your own challenge, to point out your errors in principle. But at any rate, you deprive yourself of the benefit of the above distinction by making the adoption of your principles essential to the success of your plans. You consent to the continuance of old practices, such as reading the Bible, for a time; but it is only till you can bring the whole power of your machinery to bear upon it, so as to put it down. You proceed upon the assumption that all former systems, without exception, are not only erroneous, but vicious, and destructive of human happiness. You would then act more consistently with truth and sincerity, if you would oppose them all openly and boldly, and not give your countenance to any of them for a single hour. There is only one religious system that will give you much trouble in Scotland. The teachers of it declared plainly that it was incompatible with every other. They would make no compromise with any species of error. They persecuted no man for his opinions; but they would not practise, or even seem to approve what was wrong, for a single moment. Suppose, for argument's sake, they were in error, they were at least honest ; but it is not consistent with sound principles to seem to approve, much less to pay men to teach, what you believe to be evil, and what you are labouring otherwise to counteract.

The avowed object of your second letter is, to " demonstrate that all the known systems of the world are inefficient to produce those great results, (the banishment of evil from the earth, and the universal prevalence of love and charity,) and that the new system alone can ever obtain them." We shall see by and by how this is demonstrated ; but there are two or three sentences in your first letter which require a few remarks.

" Experience," you say, " now proves that man, like all living existences, can never be virtuous or happy while he shall be constrained to think and act in opposition to his nature, or while he shall be taught to think that he can devise better laws than those of Nature. Hitherto men have been taught to think and act in opposition to their nature, and thus, and *thus only*, have sin and misery been introduced into the world."

From the former part of the same letter, we learn that the laws of Nature are your own twelve propositions, and so satisfied are you of the perfection of these laws, notwithstanding the incomprehensibility of one-third of them, that you tell us gravely that man can never be virtuous or happy, while he shall think, or be taught to think that he can devise better! Perhaps I might be tempted to agree with you, if I were in a situation in which my living depended upon " the glorious uncertainty of the law:" for I believe nothing so uncertain and equivocal in the name of law ever existed as this code of Nature enacted by you.

But the most prominent part of your doctrine in the above extract is, that sin and misery came into the world, in consequence of men being taught to think and act in opposition to their nature ; and perhaps there is more truth in this that you are aware of, or can consistently admit, according to your system. By men acting in opposition to

their nature, I suppose you mean acting improperly, or sinfully, for it seems impossible that it can have any other
meaning, since you do admit of such a thing as sin. Your
statement then is shortly this; sin came into the world in
consequence of men being taught to sin. Very well; but
who taught them? It must have been some sinful being
who was in the world before sin itself. This is a palpable
contradiction, and therefore inadmissible upon any sound
common-sense principle. I admit there is a difficulty in
reasoning upon this awful subject, and in rationally ac-
counting for the fact of sin being permitted to enter into
the fair creation of God; but it is a fact which you admit,
and which no man can deny; and I admit the truth of your
statement thus far, that man became sinful from being induced by the belief of a lie, to " act contrary to his nature;"
for the Bible which you reject tells me that " God made
man upright," and, like all his other works, " very good."
Sin therefore was not only contrary to his nature—it was
the moral destruction of it. Now there is nothing of the
nature of a contradiction in what the Bible teaches, and
what I believe, on this confessedly difficult subject. But
your system involves the absurdity of a thing being and not
being at the same time.

You take human nature as you find it in the person of
every individual as he comes into the world. You have no
idea of its ever having been in a more perfect state; and your
doctrine seems to be, that all the vice and misery of man
arise from his being *taught* to think and act contrary to the
nature in which he comes into the world. This implies
that his nature is not of itself inclined to evil; then it follows that if he were left to himself, he would not do evil;
and of course would not be miserable. Now if you
really believe this, you ought to leave nature to think
and act, and shift for itself. You admit that the
whole existing race of men are sinful and miserable in
a less or greater degree, and yet some of these are the

agents by means of whom you intend to rear, in innocence, those who are yet unborn, or who have not yet become susceptible of evil impressions. This is the most unwise thing imaginable, for it must necessarily happen, that some of the sin and misery adhering to your agents will be communicated to the young innocents; and there is no remedy for this but ordaining them to be dropt as soon as possible after they are born, and reared among their fellow-creatures of the forest.

But I am persuaded you do not believe what your words imply; for so far from leaving nature to its own capabilities, you prescribe a system of rigorous training, making it dance, and wheel, and march, when perhaps it would rather be at rest; and fiddle and laugh when it would rather weep. In short, nature is just what you think fit to impose upon the young persons who are in the unnatural state of being taken from under the care of their parents, their natural guardians, and put under the artificial training of your dancing-master, and other equally dignified functionaries.

The truth is, though you will not acknowledge it, that human nature, or rather human creatures, being in a sinful state, they cannot be either virtuous or happy till they are taught the very thing which you condemn, that is, to think and act in opposition to their nature, in your sense of the word, (that is, as men come into the world,) but agreeably to their nature in another and a higher sense, which you do not understand; and if I were to attempt to explain it, I am afraid my language would be as unintelligible to you, as some of yours is to me; for throughout your whole system, you propose nothing higher than the training of a mere mortal existence, which springs from the earth and returns to the earth, with no more prospect of a future life than the horses that draw your carriage. If such were really the condition of human nature, it would not be worth the pains which you are bestowing upon it.—I am, &c.

22d November, 1823.   W. M'GAVIN.

I SHALL occupy the remainder of this sheet with a few remarks on a letter by one of Mr. Owen's apologists, who has given his name, and is on that account entitled to more attention than any anonymous opponent. This letter, signed Abram Combe, appeared in the Glasgow Chronicle of Nov. 20th. The writer infers that Mr. Owen's system is invulnerable, because I had not attempted to dispute the truth of it in a single principle. Mr. C. had seen only my first letter to Mr. Owen, and though it had been the case that I had not got so far on my way as directly to dispute any one of his peculiar principles, Mr. C.'s inference was rather premature. But the fact is, I began in my first letter to sap the foundation of the whole system, by shewing that its first and fundamental principle leads unavoidably to absurdity or atheism. This is the most simple and direct way of disputing the truth of any principle; and if Mr. C. wishes to defend Mr. Owen's system, he must shew that my deductions from his principles were not fairly drawn. This, however, neither he nor any one else has yet attempted.

Mr. Combe accuses me of assuming the following impious absurdity,—" That the Great Controuling Power of the universe is subject to those variable feelings which seem to be peculiar to human nature." Nay, he actually gives this with marks of quotation, as if he were citing my words. But whether he was aware of it or not, this was imposing upon his readers; for there are no such words; nor any words that express such a sentiment, in that letter or any other composition of mine. From this I infer that, in Mr. Combe's opinion, imposition and misrepresentation are not improper instruments in the defence of the New System.

" Upon this absurd assumption," (Mr. Combe proceeds,) " he endeavours to push Mr. Owen to a dilemma, not on a principle of his system, but upon one of his *speculative opinions*, which speculative opinion may be either true or false, without in the least affecting the truth of the principles of the new system." Here Mr. Combe misrepresents Mr. Owen as really, though not so injuriously, as he had just misrepresented me. Mr. Owen does not propose his doctrine as a speculative opinion, but as a fundamental principle of what he calls the laws of nature, and afterwards, the eternal laws of eternal power, which he holds necessary to be understood and reduced to practice in order to the success of his system. Assuming, indeed, *his* fundamental principle, but merely as a basis of argument, I did " push Mr. Owen to a dilemma," from which no man has yet attempted to deliver him.

Mr. Combe detects me in assuming also, that there are no degrees of happiness, and that those who are not "perfectly happy" must necessarily be " perfectly miserable." I do assume, with regard to the final and eternal state of existence, that it is a state of perfect happiness or complete misery to every individual; but I assume nothing about the degrees of happiness or misery in one above another. In the present life, which is the period of Divine forbearance, there are innumerable degrees of both happiness and misery among different individuals, and with the same individual at different times; but the discussion of this did not lie in my way, in exposing the absurdity of Mr. Owen's first principle.

I am next accused of supposing that, in the new system, *coercion* is to be used to make people happy; and I maintain that so it would, if persons were put into a place of perfect purity, still retaining their impure minds; but I have nothing to do with this but to expose it as one of the consequences of Mr. Owen's principles. In the same sentence, I am accused of teaching that there are individuals who wish to be miserable. But I taught no such thing. I did not say that any creature chose misery for its own sake; but it is a fact that many choose the way of sin, which is immutably connected with misery.

Finally, it seems I am guilty of assuming that " the mere opinions of men have influence on the matters of eternity." It is needless to discuss this till we agree about the meaning of the word *opinion*. I suppose, from what Mr. Combe says of Mr. Owen, that he considers the question, whether there be a God or not, a *mere speculative opinion;* and if he does use the word *opinion* in reference to matters of such importance, I do maintain that, according as a man's opinions are in this world will be his state in eternity.

Upon the whole, it appears that Mr. Combe cannot say a word in defence of Mr. Owen's principles; and therefore he tries to find a flaw in mine. He would gladly divert me from my purpose of exposing the system which it seems he has adopted; and would put me on the defence of my own principles, which I have no objection to do in time convenient; but in the first place it becomes Mr. Owen to enter on the defence of his.   W. M‘G.

A. YOUNG, PRINTER,
150, Trongate, Glasgow.

LETTERS

ON

MR. OWEN'S NEW SYSTEM:

By Wᴹ· M'GAVIN, Glasgow.

No. 4.

TO ROBERT OWEN, Esq.

LETTER SIXTH.

Sir,

At the beginning of your second letter,
(Glasgow Chronicle, Oct. 21st,) you proceed " to prove
that it is vain and hopeless ever to expect intelligence, virtue, or happiness, from the old system of society, however
various the modifications which it has assumed, in different
ages and countries; and in the next place, to demonstrate
that the system of which the principles have been develop-
ed in the preceding letter is alone capable of conferring
upon the human race real and permanent happiness.

" A system by which this result is to be obtained and se-
cured," you tell us, " must comprehend an arrangement of
circumstances, *that shall cultivate to the utmost the physi-
cal and mental powers of each individual, and direct their
application in the most beneficial manner for himself and
for Society; that shall enable the aggregate of the species
to create, by means the most advantageous to all, the greatest amount of the most valuable products that shall affect
the preservation and distribution of these productions to the
greatest benefit of every portion of the human race; and
lastly, that shall draw forth the kindest and most benevolent*

D

feelings of our nature, and ensure to every one the best habits and conduct through life."

Then you ask,—" Has any one of the endless ramifications of that system under which men have been compelled to act, produced in fact all or any of these results? We need only appeal to the history of the past ages of the world for distinct and unequivocal evidence, that under each and all of these forms of Society, error, sin, and misery have uniformly been generated and perpetuated. And the evidence of our senses informs us that error, sin and misery are the results of each and all of them, even at this hour."

You represent the mass of mankind as acknowledging this truth. You appeal to Christendom for her evidence against the rest of the world; to Mahometans,—to Hindoos,—to the worshippers of Fo and Confucius,—and to the Jews for the evidence of each against all the world but themselves; and the conclusion which you draw from the united evidence is,—" that of all the various modifications of the old system, of which we know any thing, *not one has ever succeeded,* or *does at present succeed,* in making men either wise, or virtuous, or happy."

All that you assert here may be very true; and yet you proceed throughout upon a false assumption. By the old system you evidently mean what, in your first letter, you call, " all the systems *of the world;*" and what, in the quotation above, you call " the ramifications of that system under which men have been *compelled* to act." Now I grant that no system of the world, or worldly system ever made men wise, virtuous or happy; and because your system is a mere worldly one, and regardless of any thing above or beyond the present world, it will not be more successful than those which have gone before it, and which you condemn. While I maintain that compulsion is nec· cessary in human government, to restrain the vicious and protect the virtuous, I admit that no system under which men are *compelled to act*, can ever make them wise, virtuous or happy; and therefore I am sure your's can never do so, for the essence of it is compulsion, and nothing else, in its very first operations upon the infant body, if not also upon the mind. Virtue must be a voluntary thing, else it changes its nature, and therefore until you can find a system that will so influence the human mind, that it shall voluntarily prefer good to evil, all your labour to produce virtue and human happiness will go for nothing.

I admit the truth of another of your conclusions, that of all the modifications of the old system of which *you* know any thing, not one is able to make mankind wise, virtuous and happy. You make use of the plural pronoun indeed, by which, if you mean all mankind, you express a great mistake; but supposing you mean only persons who think as you do, I believe you assert the truth. There is an old system notwithstanding, which does produce all the good which you speak of, and a great deal more. It is not indeed one of the ramifications of any other system, young or old, though you class it with such, in consequence of your not knowing its real character. So far from being a part of the old system of the world, it is directly opposed to all the systems which worldly men ever invented, and to your's among the rest. It is very evident that you have never studied it; and therefore, as might have been expected, your " demonstration" of its inefficacy does not contain a syllable that can be justly applied to it.

You do not even honour the Christian system by a separate notice, or so much as by name, but satisfy yourself with taking it for granted that it is merely a ramification of the old system of the world; and then you introduce some things sufficiently gross and absurd, which you wish to pass for fundamental principles of Christianity.

" Conduct," you tell us again, " is the result of feelings

and opinions. If therefore, the feelings and opinions, which a system inculcates, are irrational and inconsistent, then will irrationality and inconsistency characterize the conduct of those who are subjected to its influence. Now the old system of Society is both irrational and inconsistent. For let me ask, can a system be rational or consistent, or can it produce intelligence, virtue and happiness, which impresses on the young mind the belief that man is created by a superior power, and that he cannot do any thing of himself, and that yet if he does not do a great many things of himself, he does wrong, and is to be blamed and punished here, and rendered miserable by the fear that he is to be eternally punished hereafter?"

You do not say in plain terms that the Christian system teaches this absurdity; but you put it in the form of a question, meaning it to be understood in the affirmative, that such is Christian doctrine. Perhaps you believe it to be so; but this only shows your great ignorance. I know you will accuse me of being ignorant of your system, and suppose I were so, it would not be wonderful, seeing it is but a few years since you revealed it to the world; and from the obscurity of your language, it is not properly revealed yet. But the Christian system lies fully and fairly before you, revealed in language intelligible to other men, and to you also, if you will apply your mind to it. Now I invite you to examine the whole Christian Revelation, and I challenge you to point out a passage that expresses, or even by fair construction, can be made to imply the consummate nonsense insinuated by your interrogation. But your controversy is professedly with the Church of Scotland; then I challenge you to point out a passage in her creed, or in the writings of any of her ministers, or in the creed or writings of any other Christian Church, or individual Christian of a sound mind, which teaches that man can do nothing of himself; and yet that if he do not do a great many things of himself, he is to be blamed and punished. It does not much redound to the credit of your new system that you must build it upon a false representation of the old.

Your next attempt to fix irrationality upon the old system, (meaning again the Christian,) is as follows:—" Can a system be rational which impresses on the infant mind the notion, that a being, infinitely good, wise and powerful, and who has created whatever exists, has created beings *who can think and act contrary to his will and wishes?*" In reply, let me remind you, that you admit the fact that human creatures do think and act sinfully: then it follows, according to your doctrine, either that sin is agreeable to the will and wishes of the Creator, or that man has no Creator;—or that there is no being who could make creatures capable of acting sinfully. Choose which you will, and you are again landed in atheism, or what is as bad, to believe in a God who approves of sin. It is granted, that creatures could do nothing against the will of God if he chose to prevent it; but had man been created necessarily incapable of sinning, he would not have been a free agent, or in a condition to render to his Creator voluntary service.

" Can a system," you ask farther, " be rational, that impresses on the infant mind, which by its nature can be made to receive almost any impression, the notion, that the same all-wise, powerful and good being, who knew all things from the beginning, should create a single existence that *could, by possibility, be miserable to all eternity?*" You grant that misery has existed for six thousand years; that it came into the world with sin, and is at least connected with it, for I am not sure if you admit that misery is the consequence of sin; but your admission of the fact and the connexion, is enough for my present purpose, and your question is about the rationality of the thing; and I ask you in return, to give a reason why that which is possible for six thousand years, or for a single year, should not, in the hand of Omnipotence, be possible for ever. Christianity does not teach that misery will continue in the universe longer than sin ; and as you admit the fact of the connexion in time, you cannot rationally deny the possibility of it in eternity.

Again, you ask, " Can a system be rational which, in like manner, forces on the young mind the notion, that a being with such attributes should, knowing what he was about to do, give existence to another being endowed with faculties and energies, fitted to counteract his benevolent intention, *and thus create an eternal power for the production of sin and misery?*" I answer without hesitation, that it is not rational to *force* any thing on the young mind, much less such an absurdity as this of your *creating*, which you attempt to force upon the Christian system, which knows nothing of the benevolent intentions of Deity, being counteracted by any power whatever; but which teaches, that the very opposition of the power you refer to, gives occasion for the more abundant display of Divine benevolence.

Such are a few of your *demonstrations* relative to higher matters, and thus are they disposed of. There are a few, relative more immediately to country, circumstances, and the laws of nature, &c. which shall receive due attention in my next. Now I request you to look at your demonstrations, and then ask your own conscience whether they deserve the name? You must have studied Euclid at some period of your life; and you cannot but know what demonstration is; and yet you give us as such, a series of abstruse questions, without any solution, which, proposed as demonstrations, would excite the ridicule of any school-boy, even before he had reached the ass's bridge.

The fact is, instead of studying the Christian system in the Christian volume, you have taken your notions of it from Volney and Paine, and certain French Philosophists, who knew no more of it than yourself; and who have led you into an inextricable labyrinth of absurdity. Supposing your writings and mine to be extant seven years hence, what would you say of an author who should publish an account of your system from my letters, without paying any regard to your own? In so far as I have given your own words, he might be able to give a tolerably correct statement; but still you would complain of injustice. What then shall we say of you, who do such injustice to the Christian system, as to give distorted views of it from the writings of its avowed enemies, without reference to a single sentence spoken by its author, or written by his disciples? I call upon you to treat the Christian volume as fairly as I have treated your letters. Publish the very words of it, and say what you can against them. This may be foolish; but it will be more like honesty; and in this respect, Thomas Paine was a fair adversary in comparison of you.

I am, &c.

W. M'GAVIN.

27th November, 1823.

TO ROBERT OWEN, Esq.

LETTER SEVENTH.

SIR,

I HOPE my last letter has convinced you of your error in laying certain absurdities, partly, I presume, your own invention, and partly the invention of other unbelievers, at the door of Christianity. If not convinced of error, you are at least convicted of injustice, in dressing the Christian system in a fool's coat, which enemies have shaped for her, and then pointing her out as an object of derision. I have challenged you to come forward boldly and honestly, and to tell us what you have to say against

Christianity as taught in the Christian volume, and not as misrepresented in the writing of its enemies, as you have hitherto done ; and when you have accepted this challenge, I shall be glad to meet you, and to tell you what the Bible teaches, and christians believe, in relation to some points to which you allude in the distorted representations of the Christian system, on which I animadverted in my last letter. So far as you are concerned, as an op·poser of Christianity, it is enough to have shown that your opposition proceeds upon misapprehension and misrepresentation; and that what you have given as Christian doctrine, is a gross caricature of it. To some parts of your caricature however, I admit there is an original, which, though supremely ugly as represented by you, is unspeakably lovely in itself as revealed in the Bible, and which I shall with great pleasure point out to you when I perceive you are willing to meet me on that ground.

But leaving you to ruminate on these things for a while, I proceed to dispose of a few more of your "demonstrations," as you call them, in your second letter :—

"Can a system," you ask, "be rational, which inculcates the notion, that human beings, in every part of the world, are made to be what they are, physically, mentally, and morally, by some cause, independent of that which creates their original nature, and determining the particular circumstances, in which they shall subsequently be placed?" Certainly, I answer, it would be very irrational to teach this, for it seems quite incomprehensible, and even worse than absurd, to suppose, that in any circumstances, beings can become independent of that which creates their original nature. But this has nothing to do with Christianity; and so far as I know, the old system of the world is equally innocent of it.

"Can a system be rational, which impresses on the infant mind the notion, that the laws of nature, which never change, and which are evidently the Eternal Laws of Eternal Power, ought to be resisted and opposed by human laws?" I would certainly pronounce this also very irrational, if I did not know, that these "Eternal Laws of Eternal Power," are neither more nor less than your own twelve absurd and partly incomprehensible propositions, as you assure us in your first letter; and this being the fact, I think the more they are opposed and resisted the better. What is rational and comprehensible in them, appears to far more advantage in every ramification of the old system.

"Can a system be rational, which makes it sin to act according to the laws of nature and God, and virtue to act according to human laws, in opposition to the eternal laws of nature?" Here there is such a jumble of ideas that it is difficult to give an intelligible answer. By the laws of nature I know you mean your twelve propositions; and my reply to this part of your question would be, it is very rational to oppose them, and to obey good human laws; but if by the laws of God you mean, as you ought to do, the ten commandments, I would answer just the contrary. This is the first time that the name of God is mentioned in your letters; and it clearly appears that you give his laws no pre-eminence above those of nature, which are your own twelve propositions.

As the following "demonstrations" cannot be well separated, I shall give them together:—

"Can a system be rational, which continually preaches peace, and continually practises war?

"Can a system be rational, of which the professed object is, to create union, and to cherish the kindest dispositions of our nature, while, *in practice*, it leads to universal disunion, and stirs up the worst feelings among the human race?

"Such, however, is the system which has alone governed the world through all the past ages of human existence, as far as the history of man has been transmitted to us—a system which has thus been proved to be *irrational in principle,* to be *injurious in practice,* and to be incapable, *if it were continued to all eternity,* of producing any other results than those which always have been and are now experienced by it.

"The local sytems that have obtained in limited districts of the earth, are only parts of that which has been described."

You seem to have studied no small degree of art in arranging what you mean for demonstrations. When you say " such is the system which alone has governed the world through all the past ages of human existence," it does not strike the reader at first view, that you mean the system which the Bible teaches. You do not wish to shock the world all at once with such an unequivocal avowal, but rather to insinuate it in a covert way; yet that such is your belief, will appear to the careful reader of your " demonstrations;" for it is the system that "preaches peace" that does all the mischief in the world. Now no system of *the world,* properly speaking, was ever distinguished for preaching peace. This belongs rather to the Gospel. To this then you ascribe the wickedness of continually practising war. It is the same system which you accuse of teaching the inability of man to do any thing of himself—of teaching that creatures act contrary to the will and wishes of the Creator, &c. &c. as in my last ; and which you mean for representations of the Christian system ; and this you say, " is the system which has alone governed the world through all the past ages of human existence." You will allow other systems to have had their participation in the guilt and misery of the human race, such as the Hindoo and the Mahomedan, which, like Christianity, you call " local systems, which have obtained in limited districts of the earth ;" and as these do admit some first principles in common with Christianity, such as human accountability and a future state of existence, you condemn them all as the cause of sin and misery. But the Christian system, being that which chiefly stands in the way of your improvements, is evidently the principal object of your hostility.

It is the system that teaches the doctrine of rewards and punishments, and that not only in this life, but also in a life to come, to which your system is most directly opposed; for the very foundation of yours is, that men come into the world passive compounds, incapable of either good or evil, but as they are operated upon by circumstances. This being a fundamental principle with you, you teach consistently with it, that no man deserves reward for any good which he may do, nor ought he to suffer punishment, here or hereafter, for the crimes which he may commit. It happens, that in this instance, the Christian Revelation, and the civil institutions of every enlightened people in the world, are agreed in opposition to you, only that the Bible carries the principle into a future state, while human institutions regard only the present life; but both agreeing in maintaining the doctrine of rewards and punishments, you look upon both as one system, which you call the old system of the world, which it is your avowed object to overturn.

But unhappily for the world, the Christian Revelation and the civil polity of nations agree in scarcely any thing else than the admission of this general principle, which admission it seems is enough to make you identify the one with the other, as if they were precisely they same—i. e. the one system " which continually preaches peace, and continually practises war;" but if you understood the subject, you would perceive that the preaching belongs to one thing, and the practising to another thing, which you may call systems if you please, and which in their nature are as

48

different from each other as the war is from the peace. The wars and the fightings are the effects of human corruption; the peace is the fruit of Divine mercy. Excuse the *cant* of the expression; for I am scarcely ready to speak seriously to you yet. But I venture to tell you in passing, that the Christian system is the only one that does, or ever did bring peace to men; and that it does not teach or practise war in the sense of destroying men's lives, or injuring their property, in any part of the world.

I know you will ask, whence it comes then, that wars have always been so frequent among Christians; that sometimes all Christendom has been involved in them? and if Christianity be the religion of peace, whence is it that she has not produced universal peace on the earth? My answer is, that men have not universally, or even generally embraced Christianity; no, not even the men of Christendom; and very few indeed of those who have presided over the nations of Christendom, to whom it belongs to make war or peace for their subjects. The greatest hostility against Christianity has often been, and is still practised under the christian name; and this never appears more palpably the case than when the Christian religion is made a pretext for going to war. It is not the fault of any system that it produces no good effect on the minds and conduct of those who reject it, and who act from principles which it condemns. The lovers and the makers of wars, though bearing the name of christian, are as much opposed to the doctrine and spirit of the Christian religion as those whom they call infidels; and you ought not to condemn Christianity for that which it condemns as well as yourself; besides you have had access to know, in your intercourse with society, that the practice of war is reprobated by those who have imbibed the spirit of Christianity, and scarcely by any other.

(This Letter concluded in next Number.)

ANDREW YOUNG, PRINTER.

LETTERS

ON

MR. OWEN'S NEW SYSTEM:

By W^{M.} M'GAVIN, Glasgow.

No. 5.

(Continuation of Letter Seventh.)

But I must not forget that in the first paragraph of your second letter, you assure the world that your new system "is alone capable of conferring upon the human race real and *permanent* happiness." Allow me to ask, how *permanent?* You cannot assure any individual that he will live till to-morrow; for you do not profess to save men from death; and your new system makes no provision for that which is to follow. How then can you call that *permanent,* which must terminate with regard to yourself and every other man in the world *certainly* in a few years, and probably in a few days or hours?—Supposing every other part of your system was unexceptionable, this alone inscribes perdition on its front. It is not in human nature to be really happy in the prospect of falling into nothing; and it is worse than a contradiction to say that beings to whom this must inevitably soon happen, can be *permanently* happy; unless indeed you shall teach this other absurdity, that *nothing* is the happiest of all *things!* I am persuaded you yourself could not be happy for a day, believing such sentiments as the following; contained in a letter which I

E

received a few days ago from one of your disciples, who enters very keenly upon your defence; and speaks his mind more plainly on some points than you have done: " That we are begotten without our consent, that we come into the world a passive compound, that in our progress through it we are completely subordinate to the laws of nature: in short, that we are the mere creatures of circumstances, and in the end we are hurried out of it (the world) against our will too, put into a black box, and laid in the ground; and this is the eternal round of that important two-legged animal called man.''

This young animal has not given me his name, and therefore I cannot address him directly. I request therefore that he will receive a hint through his teacher,—that when he comes to suspect that the black box will be soon preparing for himself, he may be alarmed by a *peradventure* that after all, there may be something to follow besides being laid in the ground.

I am, &c.

W. M'GAVIN.

2d December, 1823.

—————

TO ROBERT OWEN, Esq.

LETTER EIGHTH.

SIR,

I HAVE now answered all that seemed to require notice in your first and second letters. Those which follow contain little or nothing original with respect to the principles of your system, which you proceed to take as demonstrated, and to apply to practice. The principles indeed are frequently repeated and alluded to, particularly in the third letter; but a formal reply to it would lead to a needless repetition of subjects which have been fully enough discussed. It has been my endeavour to show that you have not demonstrated the truth of any one of your peculiar principles; that they are not founded in nature or fact; and that some of them would lead to atheism, absurdity, and nihilism.

I do not intend to criticise your practical details, or to controvert your statements relative to New Lanark, though I cannot allow myself to believe that it was a pandemonium before you came to it, or that it is a paradise now. I had the honour of being personally acquainted with Mr. Dale, to whom you pay a becoming tribute of respect; and knowing that he was just such a man as you say, I think it was impossible, that, with his benevolent heart and ample means, his workers could have been in such a state of wretchedness and degradation as that which you describe. Besides, I have long been in habits of close intimacy with persons who were connected with the establishment while it belonged to Mr. Dale, who have assured me, that then the utmost attention was paid to the education of the young, and the comfort of all classes of the work people. Besides, I recollect having read in some periodical publication, I think the Scotch Magazine, of a date long antecedent to your purchase of the Mills, an account of the comfortable condition of the people, many of whom Mr. Dale had brought from the Highlands, where they had been starving for want of employment, and about to emigrate, such of them as could find the means, to America. I grant, indeed, that their comfort was connected with their children being taught according to the old system, that is, to fear God, and obey their parents and masters, with the solemn prospect of a judgment to come, in which they would not be allowed to plead that they could do nothing of themselves; but would be called to account for every action which they not only could do, but had done

E 2

in the whole course of their lives. It is this kind of teaching, I suspect, that makes the old system vile in your eyes; and I would rejoice to see all our public works become, in this respect, more vile.

But I do not deny that you have made some improvements in the condition of your labourers. With such means, and with the concurrence of such benevolent men as your partners, it would have been inexcusable if you had not. The suppression of tippling-houses, for instance, was a good work, though I suspect it must have been a measure of coercion. It would have been a noble triumph for your principles, had you been able to tell us, that you had made the desire for ardent spirits to cease, and that from this cause the drinking-houses had been shut up. You do not, however, pretend to have achieved so much as this; but you did right to remove the temptation to vice as far out of the reach of your workers as you could. Many other things, I doubt not, you have done, which merit commendation, and which would have been praised by every right-minded man in the country, had you not, as is remarked by Mr. B. Gray, one of your apologists, mixed up your religious and metaphysical notions with them.

I am not sanguine about the success of your new system; and yet I confess, I would like to see it tried on such a barren waste as the moor in Motherland parish, belonging to your friend Mr. Hamilton of Dalzell—I mean your system of union and co-operation only. I would be happy to see you provide a few hundred families with comfortable houses, with domestic utensils, with mechanics' tools, with instruments of agriculture. In short, I would trust you with the furnishing of every article for their use and comfort, provided you did not attempt to furnish them a religion; or what is far worse, pretend not to interfere with the religion of any one, and yet insinuate as the foundation of your system, and as necessary in order to its success, that man should abandon their belief of Divine Revelation and of a future state, and submit to be treated as mere machines, or brutes at the best. Without this mischievous contingency, let your system be tried at Motherwell; and I hope you will live to see its inutility with regard to society at large, though the immediate effect will probably be, turning a desert into a fruitful field, to the no small delight and profit of Mr. Hamilton.

But I do not profess to interfere with any of your arrangements of that kind. My business is with the principles of your system, which you invited any man, who thought himself able for the task, to examine, and prove to be erroneous, if he could. Now I have attempted to prove you in error, by the only means which your scanty creed admits of; that is, by pushing your principles to their consequences; thus showing that they are contrary to nature and fact. I have shown that they lead to atheism, or to belief in a miserable divinity, or of one who approves of sin. I have shown that your words imply that man is a mere block, or that at best he has no natural superiority above the brute, and that he has no future existence. While you seem to teach this, you profess, by means of your system, to make the whole human race really and *permanently* happy, though falling into nothing by thousands every day! It has generally been understood, that an author is sufficiently refuted, when it is shown that his principles lead to absurdity or atheism; and I think it will be allowed on all hands that I have reduced you to the choice of one or other of these, unless, indeed, you shall prefer both.

It is possible, however, that I may have mistaken your meaning in some passages, and perhaps pushed your principles farther than you really intend that they should go. If so, I shall be happy to receive your correction, and shall cheerfully avail myself of any explanation or disavowal which you may be pleased to make ; for I assure you, it will give me great pleasure to be informed by yourself, that you do not adopt the absurdities and impieties which seem deducible from your first principles; because I am firmly persuaded that no man, who rejects the Christian Revelation, can be truly and permanently happy in himself, or the instrument of imparting happiness to others. And now having finished what I had to say in the way of exposing the errors of your fundamental principles, I intend to refute your assertion, that none of the old systems can produce virtue and happiness; which I shall do by bringing to your view a system which has done this in thousands of instances, and which is doing it every day. But in the mean time, I shall wait a week or two for your reply to what I have written; and I request that you will explicitly avow your real sentiments on the points which have been discussed. Wherever I may have mistaken your meaning, if that be the case, justice to yourself requires that you state what you do mean plainly and unequivocally.

Some of your apologists seem very willing to take the work out of your hands, if they knew how to do it; but not knowing this, one wishes me to drop the subject altogether, and another requests me to discuss the merits of the Scottish Confession of Faith, and say no more against your system till I have done so. I am glad that one of your friends at least, has been reading that venerable composition; but being, I suppose, little acquainted with the book he has gone to the wrong chapter, and given us the doctrine about the Divine decrees, which has nothing to do with the subject; whereas had he gone to the chapter about human depravity, and man's inability to please God, while in a state of sin, he would have found something more to his purpose; but I am sure he would not have found even there, what you give as Christian doctrine, " that man can do *nothing* of himself; and yet, that if he does not do a great many things *of himself,* he does wrong."

I am, &c.

W. M'GAVIN.

8*th December*, 1823.

,,,,,,,,,,,,,,,,,,,,,,,,,,,,,,,

Mr. HAMILTON of Dalzell, in a letter in the Glasgow Chronicle, pointed out a mistake in the above, which it is right to correct. Motherwell is not a parish, but a part of the parish of Dalzell; and it is not a moor, but is in general good land. That part, indeed, consisting of 40 acres, intended for Mr. Owen's Village, was a wood till about six years ago, when it was cleared and trenched. It is inferior to the other land in the district; but is considered on that account so much better for the experiment.

In the last paragraph of the above letter, I allude to some of Mr. Owen's apologists, and in particular, to one who challenged me to discuss the doctrine of the Divine decrees as held by the Church of Scotland. This, I have reason to think, was the same Mr. Hamilton, as the letter was subscribed by his initials, and was not disclaimed, but rather admitted by him, when I offered to meet him on the ground he had chosen, and called on him to say what he had to object against the Scotch Confession. There was a good deal of light skirmishing between him and me in the Chronicle, while I was waiting for Mr. Owen's reply; but it ended in Mr. Hamilton declaring off, and declining to accept of my challenge, or rather to follow up his own, for it was originally his. I was more pleased with the wisdom of this declinature, than grieved by the disappointment; for I knew I could acquire no honour by a controversy on theological subjects, with one who does not seem to know the difference between doing evil, and doing nothing. It is not wonderful that such a one should declare the Scotch Confession of Faith to be arrant nonsense throughout; but it is rather too much for him to affirm, that such is also the opinion of the greater part of the readers of the Glasgow Chronicle. I made no reply to Mr. Hamilton's last letter, because I think it unworthy of a good cause to contend for the last word; and he would be a hard-hearted opponent who would not concede that triumph to him who has no other.

TO ROBERT OWEN, Esq.

LETTER NINTH.

Sir,

A FORTNIGHT has elapsed since the publication of my last letter to you, and you have given no intimation of your intention to reply. It is probable that your avocations in London may render it inconvenient to write many long letters; but after you received the Chronicle, containing my last, in which I promised to wait a week or two, to give you an opportunity of correcting any mistake into which I might have fallen, in my review of your principles, you could easily have communicated to the editor your purpose of replying to me at such time as you might find convenient. But as no such communication has been made, so far as I know, I am left in doubt whether you mean to honour my opposition to your system with any notice. If you do not reply, I shall conclude that I have not mistaken your meaning, or misrepresented your principles on any material point; and that therefore they must bear the burden of all the absurdity and impiety of which I have convicted them.

As I do not like to be kept long in suspense; and as I always feel strongly inclined to get through with any work which I have on hand, I shall without further delay, proceed to reply to your general and sweeping assertion, that no system hitherto devised or practised in the world, has been found capable of producing virtue and happiness.

You say truly that we are born with a desire to be happy, and that we retain that desire through life. It is then a most natural question, has any man found what all men thus desire? You do not say that you have found it; and as I do not like to be egotistical, I shall not say that I have found it: but I do say, that the principles which I hold are calculated to impart it, as I shall attempt to show

by and by; and I am strongly convinced that your principles cannot confer it for one day of your life, much less
in the view of what may follow. I say what *may* follow
this life; and I do so in the way of accommodating my language to your sentiments. Speaking according to my
vocabulary, I would say, what must *certainly* follow in a
future state of existence; but you would accuse me of
taking too much for granted at this early stage of our controversy. Well, then, let it be in your way. Your system
makes no provision for what *may* follow the present life.
You have not arrived at the positive assurance that there
is nothing to follow. It is at least *possible* that there may
be a final judgment, and an everlasting state of existence.
You do not deny the *possibility* of the thing; and surely
that is the happiest system that provides against the very
possibility of danger. If I am wrong and you right, you
derive no benefit from your orthodoxy, and I suffer no injury from my mistake, for both alike die, and return to
mere dust, without any future reckoning. A disciple of
the Old System will lie as quietly in the grave, and feel
no more annoyance from the worms that devour him, than
you will do. Then supposing your system to be true, it
imparts no more happiness to you who believe it, than to
me who rejects it. But if my principles be true, even by
possibility, which you cannot deny, then the advantage
in the way of imparting happiness is unspeakably great.
They make provision for the worst, if the worst should
possibly happen. If it does not happen, I am as well as
you; if it does happen, I am safe and happy, but you are
lost and miserable for ever.

If I am wrong in taking for granted that you admit the
possibility of a future state of existence, I would then ask
if you admit the fact of a present existence? If you do
not, it is useless to have any more reasoning with you;
for you are not a reasonable being, but a mere phantom.

If you do admit the fact of present existence, you cannot rationally deny the possibility of a future one; for it is easier to conceive and understand how that which exists should continue for ever, than that it should have come into existence out of nothing.

The argument in favour of Christianity, from its affording future safety, happen what will, and of course, present happiness to all who embrace it, is, I am aware not new; for it has often been urged against infidels; but I never heard of one who could give a rational answer to it. If you can give one, I beg you will do it.

What then would you gain, and what would the world gain by the universal adoption of your principles, which you contemplate with so much complacency, as about to take place? I speak of happiness which you say the old system cannot confer, but which your new system can. You have drunk of the principles of the new system almost to intoxication. If they can make any man happy, they must have made you so.

What then is the fact of the case? I do not ask a public answer; but I request you will put the question to your own heart and conscience, and let them reply; and not only at the time when you are in full health and spirits, but when you are in sickness; or when you anticipate dissolution, which must certainly happen ere long. Are you sure that that will be the termination of your existence? and does this assurance make you happy? Then you must have a miserable existence; for on no other condition could you be happy in the prospect of its termination. This leads, you see, to a contradiction, not merely in terms, but in substance; and in fact your system is contradiction, and absurdity all over. It is impossible that you can be happy in the prospect of annihilation, else your mind is not constituted like that of any other human being; or rather you are not a human being at all. You must have a con-

sciousness of something within you different from the gross
matter of which your body is composed, and that shall survive when your body is dissolved. If your lips should
assert the contrary, your very dreams would lift up a testimony against them.

If you have gained nothing to yourself in point of happiness by your principles, it is certain the world would gain
nothing by the adoption of them. Indeed the world has
adopted them already in practice, if not in theory. Every
fool says in his heart—no God, no future state of retribution;
not that he seriously believes this; but it is the desire of
his heart that it were so; and all the world knows that
such are the wicked and the miserable, even in the present
life. In short, all the wicked in the world act upon your
principles, though only a few like yourself profess theoreti-
cally to believe them; but if all the world were both to
believe and act upon them, you would probably be convinced, even in this life, that hell is no fiction.

But there are many thousands in the world who believe
and act upon different principles. They believe in God
and in a future state; and their happiness is so connected
with this belief, that they feel conscious they would be
miserable without it. What would they gain by the adoption of your principles, even supposing them true? Certainly not more than you have gained; that is, a dreadful
uncertainty, a possibility of being lost. And what will
they lose by retaining their old principles, and refusing to
embrace yours? Nothing at all; for supposing theirs to
be erroneous, it is only an innocent delusion. Their error
does not make them worse servants, or neighbours, or
subjects; they are happy in the present life, and if there
be no hereafter, they are just as well as your system could
make them, supposing it to be true, and supposing them to
embrace it in all its extent. If therefore you have any
benevolence, which the world gives you credit for to a

great degree, abandon your pernicious experiments upon human nature, which tend to nothing but the propagation of misery in this world, and afford no hope of happiness in another.

You profess by your system to produce virtue as well as happiness, which you say none of the old systems can do; and as usual you put virtue first, as if happiness were the consequence of it, in which you do not err alone; for according to the best systems of *the world*, the virtuous only are happy, by which it is generally understood that happiness is somehow the consequence or reward of virtue. But I choose rather to reverse the expression, and to say, the happy only are virtuous. As therefore the old system of Christianity is the only one that imparts real happiness, so it is the only one that produces true virtue. The word virtue is rather vague; and, I believe, is of heathen origin, but I use it in the sense of goodness or holiness; it is acceptable obedience to the revealed will of God. This however opens a field of discussion too important to be thrust in at the conclusion of a letter, and I shall reserve it for my next.

The subject is more serious than those which usually occupy the pages of a newspaper; and while you and I have to thank the Editor of the Chronicle for the ample space in his pages which he has allowed to us both. I am happy to learn that the state of public taste and feeling is not unfriendly to such discussions, or offended by their appearance in a journal whose professed object is merely secular. Indeed there is a growing taste for serious reading, which the Editor of every well-disposed journal does well to encourage.

W. M'GAVIN.

23d December, 1823.

ANDREW YOUNG, PRINTER,
150, Trongate, Glasgow.

LETTERS

ON

MR. OWEN'S NEW SYSTEM:

By Wᴹ· M'GAVIN, Glasgow.

No. 6.

TO ROBERT OWEN, Esq.

LETTER TENTH.

Sir,

In my last letter, I endeavoured to show that your system is incapable of producing happiness, because it makes no provision for a future state of existence, but leaves men in uncertainty upon the most interesting of all questions. It must be equally incapable of producing virtue, for which it possesses neither means nor motives; and by removing the fear of punishment, it must tend greatly to the increase of crime. One great motive to virtue, is to point men to a higher state of existence; and, as they are naturally depraved, nothing can tend more to increase their wickedness, than to persuade them that they are destined to annihilation.

I proceed now to show that the Christian System, which you reject, does produce happiness and virtue;—that it is in its nature eminently calculated to do so;—that it has done so in thousands of instances, of which there is the evidence of fact;—and that it is the only one by which such effects are produced in the world. This System is called the *Gospel*, a very expressive, but to the disciples of the new philosophy a very offensive, word. I am sorry

F

to use offensive language, but there is no help for it; and it is impossible to do justice to my subject without it; for though an eminent Essayist has proposed to make the Christian religion less offensive by the adoption of a more polite phraseology, I am persuaded that while Christianity itself is an object of aversion to the unbeliever, the politest language in which it can be expressed will be an object of aversion too. Indeed, the words by which Christian truths are expressed, were originally as polite as any other, and would be so still, but for the truths themselves, to which the carnal mind never can be reconciled; and it is vain to attempt to find agreeable words to express what is in itself insufferably disagreeable.

The Gospel takes for granted what you admit, that the world is in a state of sin and misery. It finds all men, without exception, lost and ruined. It makes no difference between the Jew and the Gentile, the rich and the poor, the wise and the foolish, the master and the servant. It finds all alike lost and undone; and it comes as a proclamation of mercy, peace, and reconciliation. It does not go about to argue the matter with the sinful and miserable, or to prove by an abstruse series of reasoning, that they are miserable; but, finding the whole human race in this state, as you admit them to be, it shows to them plainly the way of happiness, and, what is more, it actually imparts happiness to every individual of the human race who embraces it.

I am aware that persons of your way of thinking, and infidels in general, suppose the Gospel to be a gloomy thing, inconsistent with the pleasures of life; and it is very common to misrepresent the publishers of it, as preachers of damnation; but this is a great mistake, or worse than a mistake, for it can hardly be ascribed to mere ignorance. The truth is, the Gospel knows nothing of damnation—it has nothing to do with it, but to save men from it. It finds men condemned, or if you please, damned already, for the whole world is *found guilty* before God, because of sin, and the sentence of condemnation is recorded; but men in general are not aware of this: because the present life is a period of respite and forbearance, and because the sentence is not *executed* speedily, the scoffer continues to laugh, the infidel to doubt, and the wicked in general to do evil, until the termination of their mortal life, when the dreadful reality is brought to view, and they suffer the execution of the sentence in all its extent. Now, the business of the Gospel is to save the condemned; and it does so, by showing a free pardon, issued from the Court of Heaven, the benefit of which will be enjoyed by all who accept of it. Christ came into the world, not to destroy men's lives, but to save them; not to call the righteous, but sinners to repentance; to seek and to save that which was lost. The Gospel finds all to whom it comes, in a state of sin and misery, which is a state of rebellion against God. It is certain, that in this state they can do nothing to please God, or to procure his favour. It is this fundamental principle of the Christian system, to which I suppose you allude, when you condemn it for teaching that man can do nothing of himself; and yet the principle is quite consistent with nature and fact. If you have an avowed enemy, who does every thing in his power to dishonour you, you would not accept of a present from that man; and though he should labour night and day, professing to serve you, while you knew that he hated you, and had only in view some selfish end, or other sinister purpose, you would never be pleased with that man's services, however laborious. Now, this is precisely the case with the whole human race, in relation to their Maker. They are sinners, as you admit. That makes them their Maker's enemies. In this state, they must be miserable, and quite incapable of doing any thing that is pleasing to Him whose enemies they are, just as your enemies can do nothing pleasing or acceptable to you; but the Gospel is a message of reconciliation. It tells the guilty and the miserable, that He who made them loves them, notwithstanding their offences; that he gave his Son to die for them; that Christ himself loved them, and laid down his life for them; and that every one who hears this message of mercy, and who believes it, is reconciled to God, receives the pardon of his sins, becomes a new man, and a happy man, and thenceforward capable of doing works good and pleasing to God, under the influence of the Divine Spirit, who is given to him, to abide with him for ever.

Sinners thus reconciled to God, are truly happy. They feel and acknowledge this not to be owing to any merit of theirs, but solely to what their Saviour did and suffered for them; and now, from a principle of love and gratitude, they obey God's commandments, which they are conscious they had never done before, because, whatever their actions might have been in the matter of them, they had never done any thing from love to God, or with a view to please him, but only from some mean and selfish principle, which must have been abominable in the sight of Him who knew the spirit and motive of every action. But now being reconciled to God, they are happy in the enjoyment of his favour here, with a confident expectation of being eternally happy hereafter: and as a life of sin is inconsistent with this happy state, and blessed prospect, they are taught and enabled to live a life of holiness, or virtue, which they never understood, or knew how to practise, before; and it is on this account that I maintain, as hinted in my last, that the happy only are virtuous.

I am aware that you do not believe a word of this. You do not even believe, that God so loved miserable sinners, as to give his Son to die for them; and I have no means of proving it to your satisfaction. I might indeed tell you that Christ himself said so, and refer you to the passages in his history where this truth is expressed in a great variety of forms; but you will not receive this as evidence; and I believe there is no sort of evidence known among men, that will satisfy you of the truth of this proposition, that "God so loved the world, that he gave his only-begotten Son, that whosoever believeth in him should not perish, but have everlasting life." If, however, you believed of yourself, what you admit to be true of mankind in general, that is, that you are in a state of sin and misery, the above would appear suitable to your condition, and the truth which it brings to view, worthy of your most cordial acceptation. As I told you in my last, you cannot be certain that sin will not be punished in a future state; and here you are told, upon what professes to be Divine authority, not only how you may escape the punishment of your sins, but also how you may have everlasting life, or be eternally happy, which your system gives you no ground to expect. If, therefore, you have any regard for yourself, you ought at least to inquire into the subject. Apply your mind seriously to the study of the Christian record, and perhaps you will perceive such marks of Divinity in it, as will supersede the necessity of any other sort of proof. You cannot be ignorant that many have done so, who in this way have been raised from a state of misery to happiness; and I am sure you cannot adduce an instance of one who repented of it.

Believing, as I do, that it is God himself who says that "Christ died for our sins, according to the Scriptures," I cannot, without great presumption, attempt to prove it by any other kind of evidence; for that would suppose the testimony of God to be insufficient. That God has given a revelation of his will, and that this is contained in the Scriptures, is another matter, and one which admits of rational demonstration; but there is no necessity that I should enter on such a work, seeing you have access to many a volume on the subject, in which the highest degrees of learning and genius have been employed. Besides, I believe it is not argument to convince your understanding that you need, so much as right principles to influence your heart, which, besides the natural bias of enmity against God, which exists in every carnal mind, has been strongly perverted by the fascination of a false philosophy. The only remedy against this, is the very thing which you dislike. It is the Gospel of the grace of God, which proclaims free salvation to sinners of the human race, without exception of any, not even of yourself, much as you have said against it. Here the character of God is presented in a light the most amiable that it is possible to imagine. He is greatly offended by your sins and mine; but he is ready to forgive all, and to save us from all the punishment which our sins deserve. This is the import of the Gospel message If you accept of it, it will impart the same happiness to you, that it has done to others; and then you will give all your wild theories to the winds. But if you continue to reject it, you must abide the consequence, which you will not be able to escape; and I know enough of human nature, to be assured that you are not happy in your own mind, when you think seriously on the subject Indeed, I am persuaded you know enough to make you very unhappy; and you will never be otherwise, unless you submit to the Gospel plan of mercy, and accept of salvation, as it is free to the chief of sinners.

In my next, I shall adduce some facts, in illustration of the subject.

I am, &c.

W. M‘GAVIN.

26th December, 1823.

TO ROBERT OWEN, Esq.

LETTER ELEVENTH.

SIR,

          In my last I stated some of the principles of
the Old System of Christianity, and attempted to show
that they have a tendency to produce happiness and virtue, which you claim as the peculiar prerogative of your
New System. In unfolding the leading principles of Christianity, it is necessary and proper that I should have recourse to the Christian record, which, at this stage of our
controversy, I have a right to take for granted as authentic,
at least so far as regards my present purpose, which is to
show the effect of certain principles upon the heart, conduct, and condition of those who embrace them. I do not
ask you to take the principles themselves for granted; but
I state them as they are in substance believed by Christians; and then I propose to show, by a series of facts,
reaching down to our own times, that these principles are
beneficial to the human race, by producing the thing which
you say no system but yours can produce.

  In proposing the principles of your system, you give no
authority but your author, whom you call Nature; and I
did not answer you by arguments drawn from Scripture;
but only from nature, fact, and common sense. You cannot, therefore, reasonably object to my referring to the authority of my author, in laying down the principles which
I maintain, and showing their influence; and I invite you
to answer them by argument, as I have done your's. I
met you on your own ground of nature and fact; and I
request you now to meet me on my ground of Scripture
and fact: or, if you prefer it, I will add my field to yours,
and meet you on the broad united ground of nature, fact,
Scripture, and common sense; according to each and all
of which I engage, if you will enter the lists with me, to

show that Christianity actually does all that you promise to do by your system, and a great deal more. But if you, after having challenged the world to argue the matter with you, shall decline to say a word in defence of your principles, I shall believe that you feel your system untenable, and hope that you will soon publicly announce your abandonment of it, so far, at least, as relates to the principles on which it is founded.

I proceed now to adduce the evidence of fact to prove what I asserted in my last, that the Gospel produces happiness and virtue in those who embrace it: and here, happily, the evidence is very abundant. Indeed, I believe there is only one other general moral truth that has so many matter-of-fact witnesses in its favour; that is, that men are sinners. This truth, which you admit, relates to the whole world; and the truth which I am about to prove, relates to all who are saved out of the world, the number of whom is, of course, smaller than the other, as a part is less than the whole; but happily the part contains so many, that no advocate of Christianity can ever be at a loss for facts to prove the blessed influence of the Gospel on those who embrace it. Unhappily for you, however, most of them are facts which do not lie within the circle in which you to choose to move, though a few of them must have forced themselves on your attention. I could bring you face to face with not a few, who would tell you that they were once miserable, but are now happy; that once they lived wicked lives, and though now they will say nothing about their virtue, their works will speak for them. But I cannot allow myself to speak of the living by name, or in such a way as would indicate any indivdual. I shall speak then of the distinguished dead; and I shall begin with one who was known to us both. It would be necessary that I should make an apology to his family, if I were referring to a private character; but the name of David

Dale is too great to be engrossed by one family. It is the property of his country, and as such I present it to you, in proof of what I maintain. He not only believed, but publicly taught, for almost half a century, the very doctrines which I laid down in my last letter, in the belief of which he lived happy, and died in the hope of happiness infinitely greater. And, as for his manner of life, both in public and private, I consider the word virtuous as coming short of expressing it. I do not say that he was perfect in temper, disposition, or in every thought, word, and deed, for the world could not contain such a one, and perfection is reserved for a higher state of existence; but he was an eminent example of industry, probity, benevolence, and almost unequalled munificence: and what is more than all, though least thought of by the world, he had the fortitude to become vile in worldly estimation, by doing good to his fellow-creatures in a way which the world despises. He began his public life in times less liberal than the present, when any deviation from established usage in matters of religion was supposed to indicate some defect or perversity of intellect. In short, when he began to preach, or, which is the same thing, to teach, in public, those truths of Divine revelation which had imparted happiness to himself, he suffered

—— " The world's dread laugh,
Which scarce the firm philosopher can scorn."

But the Gospel can do what philosophy cannot, and Mr. Dale was more than a philosopher. Notwithstanding his extensive commercial and municipal avocations, (for he was a Magistrate as well as a Merchant,) he continued to the end of life, without embarrassment or difficulty, and without pecuniary reward, to preach the Gospel, and preside in the church of which he was a pastor. Whether such a union of offices in the same individual be right, except in cases of urgent necessity, is another question, which has no connexion with my controversy with you. Mr. Dale, no doubt, felt a propriety, and even a necessity in it, as matters stood with him and his friends when the connexion was formed; and in this case, it exhibited a very unusual combination of vigorous intellect, sound principle, zeal for the glory of God, and unbounded good will to his fellow-creatures, which, together with his uniformly blameless life, and innumerable acts of beneficence, engaged the esteem of the wise and good throughout the world, and even commanded the silence of those who had not the heart to approve.

Yet, with all his excellence, I consider Mr. Dale's history as one of the weakest of my facts. His life, before and after conversion, does not present such a contrast as that of some others. He was not a profligate, whom the Gospel had reformed; but having had the advantage of early christian instruction and example, he was attentive to the decencies of life which prevail in christian society, before he came under the influence of christian principles by personal belief of the truth. He confessed himself, however, as really a sinner in the sight of God, and as much lost as any of the human race; and that his salvation was all of mercy, like that of the very worst. This confession pervaded all his ministrations, and it was his daily business to commend to others that Gospel which had brought peace and happiness to himself.

But if the case of Mr. Dale be, for the above reason, one of my weakest facts, it is, in its general aspect, a very strong one. It shows the collateral benefits which the Gospel imparts to society in general; for what system but that of christianity ever had such an effect on human affairs, not only among individuals who actually embrace it, but also in their families and neighbourhoods? The children of christian parents are not always distinguished for good conduct, but, in general, it is among them that we expect to find all that is decent, and sober, and industrious; and I am verily persuaded, that if you wanted a confidential servant, one in whom you meant to repose great trust, you would not seek for such a one in the family of one of your own disciples, but rather in the family of some christian, whose religion you despise, while you are compelled to pay it this unequivocal mark of respect. You have, no doubt, heard of the infidel poet, who had a servant who had been long in his house, and in whom he had reposed great confidence. This servant was at last convicted of stealing his plate; and in reproving him, the master asked if he was not afraid of the gallows? to which the fellow sullenly replied, You taught me to laugh at the greater danger, (that of future judgment,) and what is it to you if I choose to run the risk of the lesser one?

"How is it," says Mr. Fuller, "that in countries where christianity has made any progress, men have almost universally agreed in reckoning a true christian, and an amiable, open, modest, chaste, conscientious, and benevolent character, as the same thing? How is it, also, that to say of a man, he rejects the Bible, is nearly the same thing, in the account of people in general, as to say, he is a man of a dissolute life? If there were not a general connection between these things, public opinion would not so generally associate them." "No man thinks that genuine christianity consists with a wicked life, open or secret. But the ideas of infidelity and immorality are associated in the public mind; and the association is clear and strong; so much so, as to become a ground of action. Whom do men usually choose as umpires, trustees, guardians, and the like? Doubtless they endeavour to select persons of intelligence; but if to this be added *christian principle,* is it not of weight in these cases? It is seldom known, I believe, but that a serious intelligent christian, whose situation in the world renders him conversant with its concerns, will have his hands full of employment." " Will you dare to assert," says *Linguet,* a French writer, in an address to Voltaire, " that it is in philosophic families we are to look for models of filial respect, conjugal love, sincerity in friendship, or fidelity among domestics? Were you disposed to do so, would not your own conscience, your own experience, suppress the falsehood, even before your lips could utter it."—*See Fuller's Gospel its own witness, p.* 1, *chap.* v.; a work which I strongly recommend to your attention, and to that of all men of your way of thinking. The author was intimately acquainted with Mr. Dale, of whom I have heard him tell some interesting anecdotes. He used to say that Mr. Dale gave his money for the service of God in shovel-fulls, and that the Lord shovelled it back to him again. I am persuaded he never gave a shilling with a view to such repayment; but the fact illustrates the christian precept and promise; " give and it shall be given unto you; good measure, heaped up, shaken together, pressed down, and running over, shall be given into your bosom."

More facts in my next; meantime, I am, &c.

W. M'GAVIN.

3d January, 1824.

ANDREW YOUNG, PRINTER,
150, Trongate, Glasgow.

LETTERS

ON

MR. OWEN'S NEW SYSTEM:

By W^{M.} M'GAVIN, Glasgow.

No. 7.

TO ROBERT OWEN, Esq.

LETTER TWELFTH.

Sir,

The facts which I am to adduce in proof of the beneficial influence of the Gospel in those who embrace it, must be few, and these merely as a specimen : for were I to give you the catalogue at length, the newspapers would not be able to contain it. The few, however, which I mean to present to your view, will be such as are known to all the world ; and they shall be of a character somewhat different from the one adduced in my last. You must be acquainted (for who is not?) with the character and history of the witty Earl of Rochester, the companion of King Charles II. I mention him not only because his history furnishes a striking fact in my favour, but also because he has left on record his testimony, in the strongest language, in commendation of that religion which you condemn, and which, in the days of his folly and wickedness, he also had condemned and ridiculed.

Rochester was one of the most profligate individuals of one of the most profligate courts in the world : and he contributed by conversation, by example, and by his writings, to reduce the whole nation to a state of abandoned profligacy : but about the thirtieth year of his age his conscience was awakened to a conviction of his sin and misery. He read the Bible, and after much reasoning and great opposition from his own carnal mind, he was constrained at last to yield to conviction, which was too powerful to be re-

G

sisted, and to avow his belief of the revelation of mercy. Then he became a new man, and avowedly a happy man : and though he did not long survive to prove his new state by a new life, he did what he could to repair the mischiefs of his conduct and of his writings. He instructed Bishop Burnet to let the world know the change that had taken place in his mind, to assure his companions that he found the way of sin to be complete misery ; and that he had found happiness in what the Bible brought to his view of the mercy of God by Jesus Christ. " Laying his hand on the Bible, he would say, ' There is true philosophy. This is the wisdom that speaks to the heart. A bad life is the only grand objection to this book,' " He ordered his licentious poems to be called in and destroyed, though unhappily some copies escaped the flames; and they are still extant, to shew how just was his indignation against them, and to justify the following representation of them by Dr. Watts :

> Burn, burn, he cried with sacred rage,
> Hell is the due of every page ;
> Hell be its fate, but Oh! indulgent heaven !
> So vile the muse, and yet the man's forgiven !

See " some passages in the life and writings of John Earl of Rochester," by Bishop Burnet. Miscellaneous poems by Dr. Watts, &c.

This fact, though sufficient for the purpose of showing that the Gospel does impart happiness to the guilty and miserable, is yet not so strong as some others. Rochester died in the prime of life, of a disease that was probably the consequence of his debaucheries. His was, strictly speaking, a death-bed repentance; and though that repentance, which is connected with the belief of the Gospel, is as acceptable to God in the very hour of death as at any other period of a man's life, it does not afford to survivors the same satisfaction, or evidence of its being genuine, as that which is proved by the holiness of a life devoted to the service of God. Besides, his biographer does not seem to have himself been very well acquainted with the Gospel plan of salvation, and his dying pupil paid too much deference to his opinions; whereas, had he confined his attention to the plain testimony of Christ and his apostles, his comfort and peace of mind in his last days would have been much greater than they were.

My next example shall be that of John Newton, whose history, written by himself, is in almost every christian library. He gives a most ample narrative of his conduct and feelings while he lived among slaves in Africa, and was himself the greatest slave of all, being under the bondage of his own evil inclinations. In order to enjoy some degree of peace of mind in this state, he had recourse to infidelity. He professed, as you do now, to believe the Bible a collection of old wives' fables, but this belief could yield him no comfort in the hour of trial. But after all other refuge had failed, he found relief and comfort from the Gospel which he had despised. From being a dealer in the bodies of men, and commander of a slave ship, he became a preacher of the Gospel, in which service he continued for many years, enjoying great happiness in his own mind, and daily commending the word of God to others. He had sometimes to deal with infidels, in which he possessed an advantage, of which he did not fail to avail himself. It was, that he had at one time occupied the ground which they, and such as you, occupy now; that he knew from experience how untenable it was; and how incapable of affording peace of mind to any individual who was seriously inquiring about the way of happiness, or how he might escape the misery which flesh is heir to, or more properly, which every man of reflection is conscious that his sins deserve.

This is an example of a profligate reformed—of a miserable man made happy by the Gospel; and all this proved by a long life and peaceful enjoyment and active benevolence, of which we have the testimony of many living witnesses, as well as the evidence of his own writings. I might adduce many more facts of the same nature from the history of individuals equally known,—such as Colonel Gardner, whose life was written by Dr. Doddridge, and the late Captain Wilson, whose life, by Mr. Griffith, has lately been published. In short, as the Apostle Paul said of the worthies of ancient Israel, so may I say of the witnesses of late ages,—" time would fail me to speak of them." And I have no occasion to enter more into detail; for I am very sure you will not publicly deny the fact, that if happiness and virtue are to be found in the world, it will not be among the disciples of the new philosophy,—nor among your creatures of circumstances, but among those who read and believe, and form their lives according to the word of God.

Will you tell me what it is that has made Europe superior to Africa, and even to more refined Asia, not to speak of the savage tribes of America? and what it is that has made the British Isles, especially Scotland, superior to the rest of Europe? That there is such a superiority as that to which I refer, you will not deny; and certainly it is not because Europe has received the Gospel,—not because the British Isles, not because Scotland has received the Gospel; for alas, that cannot be said of Europe as a quarter of the Globe, and not even of Scotland as a nation. It is because the Gospel had been received in Europe, and in the British Isles by certain individuals, whose number, however great abstractly considered, has always been but small in comparison of the mass of the population. But the reception of the Gospel even by a few, in any nation, has uniformly been found to improve and ultimately to civilize those who are within the sphere of its influence. Our fathers were wild and naked savages. It was by the introduction of Christianity that they were withdrawn from the worship of stocks and stones, and from the practice of sacrificing one another to propitiate their demon divinities. The same thing is true of the other tribes and nations of

Europe. All of them have been less or more withdrawn from such savage practices ; and it would be easy to demonstrate that this has been owing to Christianity, notwithstanding the greatly corrupted form in which, for twelve centuries, it has appeared in most of the countries of Europe. Yes; Christianity stands so high above every other system, that the very caricature of it which the Church of Rome exhibits, has raised the nations of Europe, in point of civilization, far above any heathen nation on the face of the earth. How much more in those countries in which the caricature has been rejected, and the divine system received in its native purity and simplicity ! Though those who so receive it be comparatively few, they create around them a moral atmosphere, which has a happy effect on all within the sphere of their influence. It improves the state and manners of those who receive it, in the first instance, and then the effect appears in their families and neighbourhoods, of which, in my next, I may give you some facts : in the mean time I shall shortly advert to the *rationale* of the thing.

Christianity is the only system that teaches a man to love his Maker, to respect himself, and to regard the life of his neighbour. The love of God has no place in your system; and it is well that you do not even pretend to it. Christianity does not merely inculcate, it also inspires the love of God, and such love as leads to the imitation of him, for it is of the nature of love that it produces an imitation of the beloved object. Now as God is good to all, so those who love him are taught to do good to all within their reach, and the effects of this are soon seen in any neighbourhood where a few Christians are settled, whether abroad among Pagans; or at home, among those who are Christians only in name.

Christianity teaches men to respect themselves, not in the way of being vain or proud, which is the worldly sense of self-esteem, but as destined to a higher state of existence—as the heirs of a heavenly inheritance. As such they cannot live in sin, or even indulge themselves in certain practices which the world calls innocent. They live like men of a higher region, and who breathe a purer atmosphere. I speak of what the Gospel effects, when received by men in the power of it, who then become the lights of the world, and the effect is, to enlighten those who are around them.

Lastly, Christianity is the only system that teaches man to regard the life of his neighbour, and where this is wanting, there can be no social happiness. You know how little the life of a man is valued by a Turk, or a savage of any nation. You know that while a Hindoo would shudder at the thought of killing an animal, he sets no value upon the life of his fellow-man; but can rejoice in the drowning of infants, the burning of widows, and in seeing the aged die of hunger by the way side. It does not appear that, even according to your system, much as you profess to respect the species, there is any value set upon the life of individual man, and why should there be so, seeing he is a mere-passive compound of gross matter, that must soon fall into nothing? It is impossible that such a system can produce happiness or virtue among beings who are conscious that there is an immortal spirit within them. But Christianity, from the very consideration of man's immortality, and the accountability which this truth implies, teaches the value of human life, and hence it is that where Christian principles prevail, and have become incorporated with men's feelings, municipal laws, and public institutions, the life of every man is held sacred. This, I say, belongs to Christianity alone; and as there can be no happiness or virtue where little or no value is set upon human life, which I think I may take for granted, it follows as an inevitable consequence, that Christianity is the only system which can produce peace and comfort in civil society, as well as happiness and virtue in the individuals who embrace it.—I am, &c.

12th January, 1824.   W. M'GAVIN.

TO ROBERT OWEN, Esq.

LETTER THIRTEENTH.

SIR,

IT has been the object of my late letters to show that the Christian system produces happiness and virtue in those who embrace it. I admit that in the strict meaning of the words it does not produce these effects in those who do not embrace it; and it is not to blame for this, for it would be unreasonable to expect that any system should impart its benefits to those who despise and reject it. Yet the Gospel does indirectly, and to a certain extent, what we would beforehand think it unreasonable to expect. Like its Divine author, it is kind to the unthankful and the evil, and when it is cordially received by a part of the population in any country, the benign influence of it is experienced by all, inasmuch as it promotes civilization, industry, humanity, and all that is decent in social and domestic life.

For the truth of this I appealed to Europe, as compared with the other quarters of the globe, and to Scotland, as compared with the other nations of Europe. We have much vice and misery even in Scotland : but you know as well as I that these are to be found almost exclusively among the unchristian and profligate part of the people : and you cannot have lived so long in Scotland without knowing that there is a great deal of comfort and happiness enjoyed by the mass of its population, in comparison of other countries ; that this enjoyment is to be found chiefly among the serious, frugal, church-going part of the community, and that the vicious and miserable are those who regard neither God, nor the Bible, nor the Sabbath. I do not say that all the decent and apparently happy church-going people have embraced the Gospel ; but I rejoice to think a great many of them have ; and the influence of their example tells powerfully upon the rest. The natural desire, which most men feel, to stand on good terms with their more respectable neighbours, makes them imitate the sobriety, industry, and general good conduct of the Christians who live among them ; and hence it is that the Gospel, independently of its heavenly and eternal blessings, brings great temporal benefit to every country in which it is received.

But the advantage which Scotland enjoys in this respect, contrasted with her savage state, is a matter of history, not of personal observation, and therefore the impression it makes on the mind is comparatively slight. No man living has seen the transition from paganism to christianity in Scotland. But there are men alive, who have witnessed such a transition in other parts of the world, and their report confirms all that I have said on this subject, and a great deal more. Read the travels of Mr. Campbell in South Africa, and the authentic reports published every year by different societies, and you will find that Christianity has raised even the Hottentots from the filthiness and degradation which the very name conveys to the European ear, to a state of order, decency and cleanliness, almost equal to that of our own peasantry, and to a state of morals superior to the average of our city population. The following is the testimony of a young man belonging to this city, who has a temporary residence at one of the Missionary stations in South Africa, but who is not a Missionary. It is in a letter to his father, dated 1st January, 1823:—
" I am comfortably situated here, in uninterrupted good health, for which I am thankful, and although I am in the midst of Hottentots, yet I can assure you those here are a cleanly, homely, simple, social people. They are all throng (busy) building good brick houses for themselves, and we have got as good and large a school as D—— school is for them. They all wear light clothes ; and I have seen the women have day-caps of Glasgow tamboured muslin, and Paisley cotton harness shawls, spade patterns ; over gowns, I think, made of broad jaconet, Dalglish's make. And as

they are much in the same state as our fathers were in the days of the gentle Shepherd, and speaking the Dutch language, so we speak many of the same words; as for instance, gang is to go, gee is to give, kleed is clothe, keek is to spy, koft is bought, blythe is gladness, &c. &c. The Hottentots have been blamed for laziness; but being shepherds they are not so lazy as your moorland shepherds at home. *It is true they used to run naked formerly,*" &c. &c.

Here is the testimony of an eye-witness, of the change produced by the introduction of Christianity among the most degraded of our species. He says little about the religious state of the community, and it does not appear whether many or few give evidence of having actually embraced the Gospel; but the testimony is sufficiently strong as to the temporal benefits which have resulted from the introduction of it. People who formerly went naked, or were covered only with a coat of filth plastered over their bodies, are now decently dressed in cotton cloth of Glasgow and Paisley manufacture, which indicates a considerable degree of mental improvement, as well as corporeal comfort. This subject is well worthy of your attention, and that of all the spinners and manufacturers in the kingdom; and I hope it will induce them all to contribute for the support of Missionaries in heathen countries. Suppose a hundred millions of naked savages to be converted even to an external profession of Christianity, each of them would require a full dress at least once a year, which would bring such a demand for British manufactures as the most sanguine never expected to see. A christian seeks the conversion of heathens from a far higher consideration; but this is sufficient for the mere merchant and manufacturer; and the tithe of what you have spent in promoting your new view, laid out in this way, would have yielded a far better return.

Happily I am able to give an instance of civil and moral improvement by the introduction of Christianity among savages, on a much larger scale than that above referred to, and which has also taken place within the last seven years. I refer you to Captain Cook's voyages, for an account of the state of the South Sea Islands, when he visited them on his voyage of discovery. If not so filthy as the Hottentots, they were in every other respect as much or more degraded and miserable. It was the custom of mothers to murder their infants when they had more than they could conveniently rear. They were devoted to the worship of the most horrible idols, whom it was usual to propitiate by sacrificing human victims. These practices were continued to a fearful extent for more than ten years after the Missionaries from London had settled among them. But the Missionaries having at last become masters of their language, having made considerable progress in educating the young, and even obtained from some of the aged savages a patient hearing, a change began to appear in the spirit and conduct of one and then in another, which gradually spread among the people. The King, savage as he was, saw the benefit which the country was deriving from the labours of the missionaries, gave them his countenance, and at last professed to embrace Christianity himself. With the concurrence of the people, he pulled down the idols and their temples, and built in their stead houses for Christian worship, which are now crowded every Sabbath-day with sober, humane, well-dressed people. The King sent some of the idols to London, where you may see them whenever you please. He accompanied them with a letter, in which he stated his object in sending them to be, that the good people of England might see what foolish things, he and his people had worshipped as gods in the days of their ignorance.

This revolution has taken place in Otaheite, Eimeo and several other islands; and almost every month we receive authentic accounts of farther success and greater triumphs of the Gospel, not only in giving peace and comfort to the dying, but also, by raising savages from a state of rapine and misery to the enjoyment of all the comforts of civilized life. Had such a change as that in the South Sea Islands been produced by any sect of philosophers, the world would have rung with it for centuries to come; but seeing it is nothing but the ordinary effect of the Gospel, nobody minds it, comparatively few even hear of it; and perhaps this is the first time that it has met the eye of some newspaper readers.

In confirmation of what I have said above, I shall give an extract or two from Dr. Brown's History of Missions, a work which contains an immense mass of information on such subjects: " This extraordinary revolution was not confined to Otaheite and Eimeo; it extended in a short time to the neighbouring islands, Tetaroa, Tapua-Manu, Huaheine, Raiatea, Taha, Borabora and Marua, in all of which idolatry was abolished, and Christianity became the professed religion of the inhabitants. The chiefs of these islands sent repeated messages to the missionaries, entreating them to come and instruct them." " Among the other fruits which the introduction of Christianity into Otaheite and the neighbouring islands has produced, it is pleasing to witness the improvement which it has effected in the moral and civil condition of the people. The female, instead of being merely the slave of man, is now raised to a level with him as his companion. Formerly the sexes ate separately, a custom which proved the source of many and great evils; now the whole family assemble together at the same meal, men, women and children. Concubinage, which was common among the chief men in the islands, prior to the introduction of Christianity, is now unknown; and though formal marriages do not take place among the natives in general, yet the principle of the marriage union is strictly and almost universally observed. Not only has the horrid practice of infanticide ceased; but mothers who once destroyed their infant offspring, now manifest to their subsequent children a remarkable degree of tenderness and affection; and some of them deeply lamented the loss of their little ones who had fallen a sacrifice to the cruel and relentless custom."

" But though the natives have made as yet no great progress in the arts of civilization, it must not be supposed they have made no improvement. A number of them have made very neat houses for themselves, with doors and windows. They have made considerable progress in the cultivation of the ground, and now raise sugar canes, bannanas, Indian corn, water melons, tobacco, and other vegetables. They have also made public roads, and well built boats, constructed after the European fashion. The females, especially, are much improved in their habits and appearance. A considerable number of them have been instructed by the wives of the missionaries in needle-work, and have learned to make themselves neat and modest dresses. When they procure a few yards of English cloth, they do not as formerly bind it carelessly round their loins, but make it up into a gown, which gives them a much more decent appearance. They also make very neat bonnets, similar to straw bonnets; and the men likewise make hats of the same materials."—Vol. ii., pp. 315—330.

As a merchant you will ask, supposing these savages to import English goods, what have they to give in return? I answer as a merchant: there are few spots in the world which do not, if cultivated, produce something that will bring money in England; and in one year (1821, I think,) by recommendation of the King, the people of Otaheite agreed to send a quantity of cocoa-nut oil as a remittance to England, not to obtain goods in return; but as a free donation to the Society in London who had sent the missionaries, which oil sold for £1;877 3s. 7d. sterling.

I am, Sir, &c.

W. M'GAVIN.

14th January, 1824.

ANDREW YOUNG, PRINTER,
150, Trongate, Glasgow.

LETTERS

ON

MR. OWEN'S NEW SYSTEM

BY WM. M'GAVIN, GLASGOW.

No. 8.

TO ROBERT OWEN, Esq.

LETTER FOURTEENTH.

SIR,

AFTER my last was sent to the Editor, and while I was thinking of addressing you one letter more, with some additional facts, the Chronicle of Thursday last brought me your laconic and sullen reply to my former communications. Short and sulky as this reply of yours is, it furnishes an excellent refutation of your system, which it seems requires such " comprehensive powers of mind," and such " accurate habits of thinking," as no man possesses who has ventured to write against it ; and which, so far as appears, no man but yourself ever did or will possess. It is impossible that such a system can improve the condition of human beings ; seeing, by your own account, it is not level to the average of human capacity. You have not been able to communicate the understanding of it to any other man. It is therefore, in the emphatic language of an ancient patriarch, a wisdom that will die with you, so far as your fellow man is concerned ; and I suspect it will prove equally useless to beings of any other order. What I undertook to prove was, that your system could not produce virtue and happiness, or be of any real use to human

H

beings; and now your language amounts to an admission of it.

Hitherto, as you know, I have uniformly spoken of you personally in the language of respect. I have, as in duty bound, treated your principles, or what I call your errors, with all manner of freedom; but I have never descended to what are usually called personalities. You have not therefore, on that account, an apology for declining to give my letters as respectful an attention as I have given yours. Nay, you were the aggressor and the challenger in this warfare, at least so far as I am concerned. You commenced an attack against every existing system, civil and religious; and requested the calm attention of all classes, sects and parties to your letters which contained this attack, declaring it to be " the duty of those who shall be able to detect an error in any one of them, to come forward, and expose it to the public." These are your words in your letter of the 11th of October; and who would not believe that you meant to invite a friendly and serious discussion of your principles; that if they were misunderstood you would explain them, or impugned, you would defend them? Believing you pledged to this, and believing myself " able to detect" many errors in your system, I " came forward to expose it to the world," in obedience to your invitation. You have allowed me to proceed exposing it for more than two months, without a word of explanation or defence; and now you affect to have discovered that Mr. M'Gavin was not able for the task which he undertook; and you decline entering the lists with him!

This seems to be a trick of your school. Your friend and pupil, Mr. Hamilton, with a view, I suppose, to divert my attention from your errors, threw me down the gauntlet on the subject of the divine decrees, and free will. I accepted his challenge, invited him to state his objections, and promised to meet him on the ground which he had

chosen. But in an instant he turned about, declined the
contest; and to cover his retreat with a show of courage,
he commenced an attack on the Scotsman newspaper. In
like manner you turn your back upon your own principles,
to which my letters are the only formal reply that has appeared; you cover your retreat by professing your abhorrence of the Christian Instructor, to whom you are unable
to make any other reply; and then, by entering on a
controversy with some of your servants, whom you have
seen cause to dismiss, and with whom you enter the lists
very courageously, being no doubt convinced of their
ability to contend with you. In this way you abandon
your twelve laws of nature, which were to renovate the
world. You lay the blame of your retreat to my want of
understanding; but I believe the true cause is your consciousness of inability to explain or defend what I have
proved to be absurd and impious. You did not expect
to be taken up so closely as you have been; and your
extreme mortification is ill concealed under your sullen
mode of declining to occupy your precious time with what
you are *now* pleased to call "trifling."

You are not, however, entitled even to the honour of
having discovered my want of understanding, for I told
you the fact in my fourth letter. I told you that part of
your code was so incomprehensible, that I felt it impossible
to make sense of it by reading it either backward or forward, and I begged of you the favour of an explanation,
which you are bound to give, if you really believe that
mankind are to be benefited by your system. But it turns
out, either that you do not believe this, or that you do not
care about it; and then where is your philanthropy? In
this however you have proved yourself to be, as I hinted in
a former letter, a true disciple of the French school of
philosophism, of whom a great many spread over the world
about thirty years ago, which was the period of your

H 2

illumination. In the following description of them, as they appeared in America at that time, you cannot fail to discover your own picture, at least I am sure the public will discover it at once :—

" But the philosophy of the French school, with which it was intended to overwhelm these states, was in a great measure new. It was a system of abstract declarations, which violated common sense, delivered in an abstract style, equally violating all just taste and sober criticism. It is not designed to instruct or convince, but to amuse, perplex, and beguile. It is addressed, not to men of learning and understanding, the persons who should be addressed in every abstruse discussion, but to the ignorant, unthinking and vulgar. It is directed, not to the understanding even of these, but to their weaknesses, prejudices, and passions. The language in which it is uttered, like the signs of unknown quantities in algebra, is without meaning, until you arrive at the result, and the application; and it is never designed to come to a result, or admit of an application. *If you answer an argument, or a book, according to its obvious meaning, you are gravely told that you have mistaken the author's intention. When you inquire for that intention, you will be left without an answer, or will receive one in the very language which you are declared to have mistaken.* Proceed a few steps farther, and you will find yourself in a labyrinth, compared with which that of Minos was a beaten high way. The doctrines really intended to be taught by this philosophy, are like the furniture stowed in the paradise of fools,

Abortive, monstrous, and unkindly mixed.

The principles upon which they apparently rest, are mere hypotheses; *destitute of any foundation, and without any authority, besides the egotism of the author.* The arguments by which they are professedly supported, are usually of the *a priori* kind ; attended with no evidence, and conducting the mind to no conclusion. Were they delivered in language capable of being understood, their authors would be considered as the Newtons and Aristotles of folly. At their side, Behmen and Swedenborg, those laureats in the ' limbo of vanity,' would lose their distinction, and return far towards the character of common sense."—*Dwight's Travels*, vol. iv. p. 374, *New-England edition*, 1822.

This system, ridiculously absurd as it is, had for a time a pernicious influence upon the religious character of the youth of New-England ; but it was ultimately put down by the good sense of the descendants of the English puritans ; and I am persuaded it cannot stand much longer before the good sense of the Scots, who, though somewhat slow in their movements, are pretty sure in the end. My object has been, to hold up the system to the world, in its naked deformity ; and I know very well that I have not laboured in vain. I have reduced you to a virtual abandonment of your fundamental principles, when you declare that you will not defend them ; because, as you tell us, you have matters of too great moment before you, *to waste your time in trifling.* I believe my time is as much occupied with matters of moment as yours ; but I am determined to persevere in exposing your errors, whenever you shall broach them again ; and to defend the truth which I have exhibited in opposition to them : and you may call me a traitor to my own cause, when you find me shrinking from the work, under the hollow pretext that the matters in dispute are trifles ; or that the defence of the truth in any form is trifling.

It was easy to discover, it seems, from a few sentences in Mr. M'Gavin's " first letter, that he had entered on a task greatly beyond his present attainments. The subject comprehends whatever relates to the permanent well-being of society; and for a discussion and investigation of this nature, it is evident that Mr. M'Gavin does not possess the requisite experience or mental qualifications." This is a subject on which, you are aware, you may assert what you please, without extorting a reply from me. I admit that your assertion would have been true, had I professed to understand, or undertaken to explain, your system. But this was not the case. I undertook to disprove your assertion, that none of the old systems could produce virtue and happiness, and that yours alone could do it. Without pretending to understand your system, I found that in your development of it, you expressed sentiments absurd, contradictory, which led to atheism; and which, in the nature of things, lead not to happiness, but to misery. This I have shown to the world; and you cannot deny it. You dare not attempt to explain or vindicate your sentiments; for you know that you cannot, without confirming the truth of my representation of them. Here I will join issue with you, whenever you please. If my mental attainments are low, you have the better chance of confuting me. If you decline this challenge, you tacitly admit having broached the most absurd nonsense and impiety, without having fortitude to defend it, or grace to acknowledge it, when pointed out.

On the other hand, I have shown you an old system that does produce happiness and virtue; which is proved by innumerable facts. I challenge you to combat the principles; and disprove the facts, if you can. If you shall also decline this, I shall hold the truth established, and your assertion refuted; and have no doubt of obtaining a public verdict to the same effect.

I am, &c.

W. M'GAVIN.

20th January, 1824.

TO ROBERT OWEN, Esq.

LETTER FIFTEENTH.

Sir,

Your long letter in the Chronicle of the 17th
instant, in reply to certain of your servants whom you have
dismissed, shows that you have no fixed purpose of not
replying to an opponent, when you find that you can do
it. Some great authors have laid down a rule, and per-
tinaciously adhered to it, that they would not reply to any
opponent whatever; so that the world never knew when
they were, and when they were not, convinced of their
errors. But you have not bound yourself by such a rule.
You are as ready as any man to defend yourself when you
think you have tenable ground and had you been able to
make as good a reply to the Christian Instructor and to
me, as you have done to your late servants, you would not
have put us off with a sneer of contempt and pity for our
ignorance and obduracy.

Since writing my fourteenth letter, I have yours in the
Chronicle of the 20th instant, which confirms, in every
point, the character of the French infidel school, as given
by Dr. Dwight, and quoted and applied to you in my last.
I exposed the leading principles laid down by you, as absurd and partly unintelligible. You gravely tell the world
that I misunderstood your intention. I called upon you
to explain yourself. You refuse giving an explanation;
and now you come forward and repeat the same incomprehensible jargon, in nearly the same words which you
say I misunderstood. You affected at first to stand so
very high that you would not dishonour yourself by de-
scending to answer Mr. M'Gavin; but this last letter of
your's is the fruit of an after-thought. It is meant as an
answer to him, though you do not say so. You do not
mention his name, or refer to any part of his letters; but

as their general scope was to exhibit the Christian System in opposition to yours, you have made a last and desperate effort to press Christianity into your service, and to make it appear on your side; which shows that I have brought you to entertain a better opinion of it than formerly; for in what you call the development of the principles of the New System, you speak of every modification of the old one, evidently including Christianity, as producing nothing but error, sin and misery; and incapable of producing any thing else, though continued to all eternity.

You have quoted so many passages of Scripture, and said so many fine things about the millennium, and loving one another, that no doubt you will be set down as a very religious man, by people who do not know the difference between truth and error; such, for instance, as her *royal highness* the Princess Olive of Cumberland, who published under her *royal* hand, in the London papers, a few months ago, a certificate of your good religious character; declaring her belief that you had no dislike to Christianity, but only to certain professed teachers of it, whom, with a perversion of Scripture almost as absurd as yours, she described as *sheep* in *wolves'* clothing,—omitting however to tell us what would be the use of the wolf's coat to a sheep without also the tusks and the claws.

To those, however, who understand the subject, it will appear that Christianity is more insulted by your professed alliance than your avowed hostility. Your respect for it is precisely that of the Pagan to his Maker, when he makes an image of him. His conceptions of Deity rise no higher than the image, and he knows nothing of the God of the Bible. So your Christianity is not that of the Bible, but a mere, and a very gross image of it, the creation of your own fancy. I described the Christianity of the Bible in my tenth letter, and need not repeat it here. The main object of it is to save men from sin. It relates chiefly to the soul of man, and to his future state of existence. But your system, and the Christianity which you would attach to it, have no relation whatever to a future life. Your Christianity rises no higher than digging, building, spinning, weaving, eating, drinking, sleeping, and annihilation; and you have the astonishing presumption to "call upon *all Christians* to bend their minds to this subject, to make themselves masters of it," &c., and then, of course, to admit that such is Christianity, that your system is its most powerful auxiliary, and at your bidding, without a word of objection, to abandon their hopes of heaven, and rest satisfied with a corner of some earthly paralellogram; for if any one should whisper an objection, you would scorn to give an answer, and pronounce the unhappy individual destitute of the powers of mind necessary to understand or enjoy your new and millennial state.

That your Christianity is such as I have here described, is evident from your assertion and your admission. You assert throughout that your system is incontrovertible and demonstrable truth. You admit now that Christianity is also true, and you say truly that every truth must be consistent with every other truth, therefore, Christianity is a system that regards men as mere brute matter, or passive compounds, having no activity in the formation of their own character, deserving neither praise nor blame for their good or evil actions.

But that such is your Christianity rests on stronger evidence than mere inference, for you assert it as plainly as you can assert any thing. "The single base," you say, "upon which the new system rests, is, that the character of every human being is formed *for* him." "Is it contrary to Christianity that the infant has no merit or demerit for the good or bad qualities which his Creator has given him at birth?" What you here put in the interrogative form, you mean, of course, as an assertion that this is not contrary to Christianity. Again, you say, "In short, the Scriptures most distinctly and unequivocally tell us that the individual forms no part of himself nor of his character, which is in every instance the direct work of his Creator." I have to thank you now for being plain and intelligible, at least in those three passages which I have extracted. The infant, it seems, receives both his good and bad qualities from his Creator; and in after life the individual has no more to do in forming his character than in creating himself; both in *every instance* are the direct work of his Creator. This is Christianity as you understand. This is what "the Scriptures most distinctly and unequivocally tell us." You cite a number of passages, but not one of them says any thing like this. The impudence of the, Pope of Rome, when he calls himself the vicar of Christ and God on earth, is modesty in comparison of yours, when you palm such absurdity on the Bible; for the Pope is ashamed to have his arrogance brought into contact with the Bible, and therefore he forbids the general reading of it; but you support a school in which the Bible is read; and to the public of Scotland, who have the Bible, and read it every day, you have the effrontery to assert that the Bible teaches distinctly and unequivocally what is condemned with abhorrence in almost every page of it; namely, that God is the author of evil; that he gives to infants their *bad* qualities, as well as their good ones; and that *in every instance* He is *directly the former of the human character*, however depraved; such, for instance, as it appeared in Judas Iscariot, and Thurtell the murderer! This is your Christianity; and, if possible, it is worse than atheism.

Now, you must not sneer me off again, as wanting a capacity to understand your system; for your language here is so plain that it is impossible to mistake your meaning.

You have ventured to appeal to Scripture; and you quote several passages which assert that God is the Creator of our persons, and the author of all that is good in us. This is what every Christian most firmly believes. But you bring forward these texts to prove that God is also the author of all that is evil in man; of which not one of them gives the slightest hint. The language of Scripture is, that " God made man upright, but he sought out many inventions:" in other words, all that is good in us is of God, and all that is evil is of ourselves.

I see you are as sanguine as ever about the success of your plans. " This very year," you assure us, " will the practice be commenced, which will hasten the period ' when swords shall be turned into ploughshares, and spears into pruning-hooks;' when every man will be placed under those new circumstances, in which he may ' sit under his own vine, and his own fig-tree, and none to make him afraid;' and when, in reality, ' there shall be but one language, and one people.' " " How certain! how beautiful! and yet how simple! are the means by which the great Author of all things will effect this mighty change! All human resistance is rendered absolutely powerless. He gives to mankind the knowledge, that the character and conduct of the individual can never be formed by himself, but that it ever must be formed *for* him, by the circumstances which others place around him." Why, you told us just now, that the formation of individual character is, *in every instance*, the *direct* work of the Creator! Here, you make it the work of circumstances; which circumstances are placed around the individual by his fellow-men! And it is the knowledge of this palpable contradiction, that is to begin this very year to regenerate the world! This is the fulcrum on which you fix the lever that is to move the globe;—and I am verily persuaded, that if you understood your own meaning, you would not venture the weight of your foot upon it.

Great projectors, however, are usually great enthusiasts; and enthusiasm will sometimes do more than common sense. I expect, therefore, to see your village built and peopled in a year or two; because that is what men and money can accomplish. But as you have no means of regenerating the people in a religious and moral sense, you will leave them, in respect of real and permanent happiness, just as they were. If they shall be regenerated and made happy, it will be by means of the Gospel, which is as accessible to every other village in the kingdom as it will be to yours;—and unless a happy change shall take place in your own mind, I would dread a counteracting influence in your village, that would obstruct rather than further the real happiness of the people.—I am, &c.

W. M'GAVIN.

24th January, 1824.

———

HERE, for the present, I close my correspondence with Mr. OWEN. His refusal to explain or defend the principles of his system, after having challenged an examination of them, is a tacit admission that they are untenable; and it is neither honourable nor profitable to continue a contest with the vanquished. He has published several letters since my last was before him; but he makes no allusion to any thing that I have written, and scarcely any to his own fundamental principles, whose absurdity I exposed;—from which it may be inferred, that he will in future be silent on these points; which is as much as I expected to gain by my exposure. I never professed to criticise his practical details; and while he confines himself to squares and parallelograms, he shall receive no molestation from me. If, however, he shall again insult the common sense of mankind, by publishing such atheistical reveries, I shall be ready to repeat my exposure of them.

W. M'G.

ANDREW YOUNG, PRINTER,
150, Trongate, Glasgow.

MR. OWEN'S ESTABLISHMENT,

AT

NEW LANARK, A FAILURE!!

AS PROVED

BY EDWARD BAINES, ESQ. M. P.

AND OTHER GENTLEMEN, DEPUTED WITH HIM

BY THE PARISHIONERS OF LEEDS,

TO VISIT AND INSPECT THAT ESTABLISHMENT,

AND REPORT THEREON.

"Mr. Owen's establishment is conducted in a manner superior to any other the Deputation ever witnessed, dispensing more happiness than perhaps any other Institution in the Kingdom."
"Public Houses, and other resorts of the vicious are no where to be found in this happy village.'
"Intoxication, the parent of so many vices and so much misery is indeed almost unknown here.'
"No cursing or swearing is any where to be heard."
"There are here no quarrelsome men or brawling women."
"The inhabitants of this place form a more Religious Community than any other Manufacturing Establishment in the Kingdom."

MR. BAINES' REPORT.

PRICE ONE PENNY.

Leeds

PUBLISHED BY THE LEEDS DISTRICT BOARD OF THE ASSOCIATION OF ALL CLASSES OF ALL NATIONS, OFFICE, WALTON'S MUSIC SALOON, SOUTH PARADE.

1838.

INTRODUCTION.

WHEN the friends of Social order and Rational Christianity submit their view of that state of society which is alone calculated to ensure universal happiness, to general investigation, and call for argument, they are invariably met by a demand for *precedent*. The wedded partizans of the present irrational system, (refusing to argue the question of probability, or to follow them in their deductions of consequences from principles) cry out, unanimously, " shew us that such a state of society has yet existed." We readily admit that, in its fullest extent, we are unable to do this. There has never, within the compass of known history, existed a perfectly rational state of society—but several approximations thereto have been made ; such as proves sufficiently the soundness of the data whence our conclusions are drawn. We point our enemies to the Essenes among the ancient Jews; to the Primitive Christians in the time of the apostles; and to the various establishments of the Rappites and the Shakers in America, not as perfect samples of the workings of our economic principles, but as evidences of their capability to ameliorate and improve the human character beyond any others ever known or acted on. But these are all too long gone by, or too far off, and nearer and more recent evidence is asked for. We point to the establishment of Mr. Owen, at New Lanark ; and are at once told with an unblushing front that that establishment is known to have been a failure. It might reasonably have been thought sufficient to rebut this naked assertion by the counter assertion of Mr. Owen, and others, who knew all the circumstances connected with that establishment, so thoroughly that they cannot have been deceived, and whose moral character is above even the suspicion of a wish deliberately to deceive others. The advocates of the rational system, however, fortified by stronger proofs than were probably ever known under similar circumstances, ask no credit for their statements, further than as they are corroborated by the concurrent testimony of others, who, with character equally high and uncompromising, cannot be suspected of any partiality for Mr. Owen's system or principles : hence, therefore, they refer with pride, and earnestly entreat attention, to the following report, made by gentlemen utterly unconnected with them, or with Mr. Owen, and whose views of the Constitution of Society are known to be widely different.

REPORT, &c.

THE DEPUTATION appointed by the Guardians of the poor of the township of Leeds, to visit the establishment of Mr. OWEN, at New Lanark, beg to report to their constituents,

That they left Leeds on the morning of Thursday, the 26th of August, and that they arrived at Lanark on Saturday in the same week.

After remaining at that place till the Wednesday morning following, they repaired homewards, and arrived in Leeds on Saturday evening, the 4th of September, having been absent ten days.

On their return to Leeds, they spent one day with Mr. FALLA, at Gateshead, near Newcastle, where they received from that gentleman some useful information on the subject of spade husbandry, the result of which they deem it a part of their duty to communicate.

In submitting this report, their first duty will be to give a general view of Mr. Owen's establishment as at present constituted; then next to show wherever it differs from that species of establishment which he so forcibly recommended in his lecture at Leeds; and the last, to suggest how far, according to their views, Mr. OWEN'S plans, combined with Mr. FALLA'S system of spade husbandry, may be made conducive to the two great objects of public interest—the reduction of the poor's rates, and the increased comfort of the necessitous poor.

Previous to their departure from Leeds, they were furnished by the committee with a number of questions, the answers to which will be found in the book which accompanies this report.

The information contained in these answers serves to show the nature of the establishment at Lanark as it at present exists, and in this branch of their duty, it will be mainly important to show its effects upon the inhabitants.

Mr. OWEN'S establishment at Lanark is essentially a manufacturing establishment, conducted in a manner superior to any other the deputation ever witnessed, and dispensing more happiness than perhaps any other institution in the kingdom where so many poor persons are employed, and is founded on an admirable system of moral regulation.

The population of the village of New Lanark, the whole of which is attached to Mr. OWEN'S concern, consists of 2293 individuals, exclusive of which there are 188 persons employed in the Mill from Old Lanark: of this number there are 103 under the age of two years, and 380 between two and ten years of age: these latter are receiving daily instructions in the schools, and by showing to them a spirit of kindness, and impressing them with a sense of their duty, (without the hope of reward or the fear of punishment) they are making satisfactory progress in reading, writing, and accounts, as well as in music and dancing, in addition to which the girls are taught to sew. In the education of the children the thing that is most remarkable is the general spirit of kindness and affection which is shown towards them, and the entire absence of every thing that is likely to give them bad habits—with the presence of whatever is calculated to inspire them with good ones ; the consequence is, that they appear like one well regulated family, united together by the ties of the closest affection. We heard no quarrels from the youngest to the eldest, and so strongly impressed are they with the conviction that their interest and duty are the same, and that to be happy themselves it is necessary to make those happy by whom they are surrounded, that they had no strife but in offices of kindness. With such dispositions, and with their young minds well stored with useful knowledge, it appeared to us that if it should be their destiny to go out to service or to be apprenticed, the families in which they are fixed would find

them an acquisition instead of a burthen, and we could
not avoid the expression of a wish, that the orphan
children in our Workhouses had the same advantage
of moral and religious instruction, and the same prospect of being made happy themselves and useful to the
families in which they may be placed. Whenever this
shall be the case, instead of the Town finding it difficult
to get masters for these children of poverty, they will
rather be sought for than despised, and instead of rising
into manhood with expectation of relying upon a parish
all the days of their future life for a portion of their
support, they will feel an ambition and a capacity to
maintain themselves.

The next class of the population in the Lanark
establishment consists of boys and girls between 10 and
17 years of age. These are all employed in the mill,
and in the evening from seven to half-past eight o'clock
they pursue that system of education to which their
attention has, up to 10 years of age, been directed in
the day time. The deportment of these young people,
owing, probably to the advantages of their early training, is very exemplary. In business they are regular
and diligent, and in their manners they are mild and
engaging. They are taught to know that vice and
happiness can never be long allied, and they seek their
gratifications rather in the improvement of their minds
than in the company or in the habits of the dissolute.
Public houses, and other resorts of the vicious, are no
where to be found in this happy village, and the absence of their contaminating influence is strikingly exemplified in the contrast of manners and of conduct
between the inhabitants of New Lanark, and, of most
(we fear we may say all) other manufacturing places.
It is proper here to observe that from the nature of Mr.
OWEN'S establishment, employment cannot be found in
the Mills for all the boys born and educated in the place,
and on that account many of them, when they have
finished their education, are placed by their parents at
mechanical or handicraft trades. What has been the
conduct of any considerable number of these boys when

A

they are removed from the moral restraints of their former situation it was not in our power to ascertain, though we have little doubt but the advantage of their early education will be felt upon their moral habits in every period of future life.

In the adult inhabitants of New Lanark we saw much to commend. In general they appeared clean, healthy, and sober. Intoxication, the parent of so many vices and so much misery, is indeed almost unknown here. The consequence is that they are well clad, and well fed, and their dwellings are inviting. The Scotch character has in it, no doubt, something that disposes to a more exemplary observance of the Sabbath than is generally to be met with in England ; but this circumstance apart, it is quite manifest that the New Lanark system has a tendency to improve the religious character, and *so groundless are the apprehensions expressed on the score of religion suffering injury by the prevalence of these establishments*, that we accord with Mr. OWEN in his assertion that *the inhabitants of that place form a MORE RELIGIOUS COMMUNITY than any manufacturing establishment in the united kingdom.*

This effect arises out of the circumstances by which they are surrounded, and is wholly independent of any sentiment on religious subjects entertained by Mr. OWEN himself. Instead of the work people of Lanark spending their evenings in the public house, many of them derive their amusement from witnessing the performances of their children in the school-rooms. In this well regulated colony, where almost every thing is made, wanted by either the manufactory or its inhabitants, no cursing or swearing is any where to be heard.

There are no quarrelsome men or brawling women. These effects arise partly out of the moral culture of the place, partly from the absence of public houses, as we have before said, and partly from the seclusion of the inhabitants from the rest of the world, if that can be called seclusion where 2,500 persons are congregated within the narrow compass of a quarter of a square mile.

High wages it is quite manifest are not the cause of
the comfort which prevails here. Amongst us their
earnings would be thought low. The wages of those
under 18 years of age, per week, are, for the males that
work by day, 4s. 3d.; for the females 3s. 5d.; and for
those that work by the piece, 5s. 4d. for the former,
and 4s. 7d. for the latter. The average weekly wages
of those above 18 years of age are, for men, 9s. 11d.;
for women 6s., by the day; and 14s. 10d. for the
former, and 8s. for the latter by the piece.

In addition to the above there are about 240 women,
(chiefly heads of families) employed partially in picking
cotton, whose earnings amount to an average of 2s. 8d.
per week. Every person in this establishment contributes one sixtieth part of his wages to a common
fund, which is appropriated to his relief, in the time of
sickness, besides which there is a savings' bank for the
work people, whose deposits as taken last Christmas,
amounted to £3,193 14s. 10d. The moral habits of
the people are, as we have before stated, very exemplary, and this assertion will receive additional confirmation from the fact, that although there are in the
institution 1,380 females, there have been only 28
illegitimate births during the last nine years and a half,
and the fathers of those children have been chiefly
non-resident interlopers.

Having thus given a view of the situation of the
inhabitants of New Lanark, as arising out of the system
which at present prevails there, we next proceed to contrast that system with the state of society which MR.
OWEN recommends, and some of the characteristics of
which he is at present gradually introducing. We
have already said that the present institution is a manufacturing establishment. Mr. OWEN recommends that
the new villages should be principally agricultural.
He has at present only 240 acres of land, including 90
acres which are rented, and that for a population of
about 2,500 persons; while, from the difference of the
circumstances, he recommends that there should be
1000 acres for 1,200 individuals. At present every

family has its own earnings, and appropriates them as they think proper: he recommends that there should be a community of interests, and that they should have all things in common. The construction of the present village is not accordant with that he recommends; he proposes that the erections should be formed into squares, but the houses at New Lanark are in one part of the village in streets, and in another in a row, forming rather an irregular oblong square with the mills. The system of education and moral culture which at present exists, and which may be said to form the foundation of the fabric, is pretty similar in his present plan to that he recommends. The children are instructed gratuitously, and pay only the trifling sum of three-pence per month for books, pens, ink, and paper. There is, however, this difference—at present none of the children are set to work till they attain the age of ten years; but on the new plan they would begin to work in the open air, one hour in the day, at six years of age, and increase one hour every year up to 12. Such are the leading characteristics in contrast of the present plan and of that which Mr. OWEN proposes to adopt in any village founded on his plan. As far as he has advanced, which he says is only two points towards twenty, supposing the latter to be the number of perfection, he has effected great things, more than could have been anticipated.

It only remains for us now to suggest how far Mr. OWEN's plans, combined with Mr FALLA's system of spade husbandry, can be made conducive to the permanent reduction of the Poor's Rate in this township, and to the improvement of the condition of the necessitous poor. This is by far the most arduous part of the duty of the deputation, and when the legislature of the country have laboured for years on this subject, without producing any beneficial result, great allowance will be made on account of the difficulty of the undertaking.

It will be observed that our enquiry has been undertaken solely for parochial purposes, and that, in making this report, we do not enter into the general subject of the advantages of Mr. OWEN'S system as a national measure.

There can be little doubt that if an agricultural colony, similar to that recommended by Mr. OWEN at Leeds, could be formed here, great public benefit would accrue from its establishment. This observation must, however, be taken with some limitations:—The community of interests involves questions of great difficulty, and as that state of society has seldom been tried in any, and never in a pauper population, we must beg, for the present, not to offer any opinion upon its expediency.

It would have been very satisfactory if the experiment establishment on Mr. OWEN'S plan, as resolved upon at the meeting at which the Duke of Kent presided in London, last July, had been formed, as the success of that institution would have inspired confidence in the friends to the system both in Leeds and other places. But we understand that the subscription set on foot for that purpose languishes, and that Mr. OWEN'S presence will be necessary to impart to it sufficient animation to consummate the undertaking. Under these circumstances considerable delay must arise, and it will remain for the inhabitants of this place to determine whether they will wait to witness the result of that incipient experiment, or they will take the risk and the honour of originating an agricultural village in the neighbourhood from the resources of the township of Leeds.

To effect this purpose considerable funds would be wanted, though if the land be rented on a pretty long lease, instead of purchased, much less than the amount mentioned by Mr. OWEN would be required, perhaps £40,000, (instead of £100,000) would be sufficient to build the village and stock the farm. It would, however, be necessary to have the sanction of two important bodies before any material step could be taken in the business—a Vestry Meeting of the inhabitants of Leeds, and a legislative enactment to authorize the persons engaged in the business to raise the supplies, and to apply them to the proposed purpose. In the course of the next session of parliament, Sir Wm. de Crespigny and other members of the legislature will probably bring the subject under the consideration of the senate, and in the interval the London Institution will be advancing towards its completion. With the light derived from these sources the guardians of the poor in Leeds will be enabled to regulate their future conduct; without such aid the deputation, (however strongly impressed themselves with the benefits that will accrue to all parts of society by the introduction of Mr. OWEN'S plan) could not feel justified in taking upon them the responsibility which would attach to urging forward a measure involving such important and complicated interests.

In the meantime the distresses of the poor are pressing, and the demand upon the parochial funds are unexampled at this period of the year. Some temporary expedient is therefore rendered necessary, and from the experiments made by Mr. FALLA, an eminent nurseryman of Gateshead, in a system of spade husbandry, it appears that labour may be found for the unemployed poor in that way, and that the abundance of the crops will reward, and more than reward, the extra labour bestow upon the ground by substituting the spade for the plough

In the neighbourhood of Newcastle, where these experiments are made, the average produce of land, by plough husbandry, does not exceed 30 bushels an acre; but on the small quantity of land which Mr. FALLA has this year cultivated by the spade, he has produced by sowing:—

In the broad-cast way....58⅔ bushels per acre.
9 inch lines drilled .....65⅔   do.
12   do.   transplanted 61   do.
6   do.   do.   62½   do.
9   do.   do.   56¼   do.

From which it appears, that the most productive experiment is that made in 9 inch lines, by the drill mode of sowing, and Mr. FALLA recommends this

system in preference to transplanting, which, though it
saves seed, does not produce an adequate remuneration
for the additional trouble and expense. The average
produce of the spade over the plough husbandry, on
land of the same kind, and of the same degree of rich-
ness, is therefore, at the least, 30 bushels an acre ; and
the advantages of that system are thus exemplified :—

Digging per acre	£2	0	0
Drilling	0	6	0
	2	6	0
Deduct two ploughings	0	16	0
	£1	10	0

Additional produce :—30 bushels, at 9s.	£13	10	0
Extra expense as above	1	10	0
Balance	£12	0	0

If these calculations be correct, and they are founded
upon actual experiments, made for three successive
years, by a practical agriculturalist, it follows that there
is a balance of twelve pounds per acre, in favour of
spade husbandry, after affording to the workman two
pounds worth of human labour on each acre of land.

With these results before them, the deputation do
not hesitate to recommend, that a sufficient quantity of
land should be taken in the neighbourhood of Leeds, to
employ a portion of at least their unemployed paupers,
and as the period for digging is approaching, that no
time should be lost in securing the land. The impedi-
ment arising out of the act of parliament, which does
not allow parishes to take more than 20 acres of land,
may be obviated by a few spirited individuals taking a
portion of land in the neighbourhood. Persons of this
description, they apprehend, will readily be found; and
the able-bodied poor will thus be supplied, without any
expense to the parish, with what they so much want—
Labour and Bread.

Another object that the deputation would earnestly press upon the committee, is the placing of the orphan children, at present in the workhouse, under a system of moral culture somewhat resembling that which prevails at New Lanark. The number of these children, at present in the house, is 29 boys and 21 girls. The difficulty of obtaining for them masters has become almost insurmountable, and too many of these, for want of a proper training, when they go out into the world, are pests instead of blessings to society. To effect an object so salutary, it is desirable that they should be placed at a distance from the contaminating influence of the society of the adult paupers—that their minds should be trained to virtuous inclinations—that their health should be watched over—and that they should have a good plain useful education, suitable to their humble situations in life, and calculated to render them an acquisition to any family in which they may be placed.

With this recommendation the deputation closes its labours, and they trust that they have not been wholly in vain.

EDWARD BAINES.
ROBERT OASTLER.
JOHN CAWOOD.

Leeds, Sept. 14th. 1819.

Joshua Hobson, Printer, 5, Market Street, Leeds.

British Labour Struggles:
Contemporary Pamphlets 1727-1850

An Arno Press/New York Times Collection

Labour Problems Before the Industrial Revolution. 1727-1745.

Labour Disputes in the Early Days of the Industrial Revolution. 1758-1780.

The Spread of Machinery. 1793-1806.

The Luddites. 1812-1839.

The Spitalfields Acts. 1818-1828.

Friendly Societies. 1798-1839.

Trade Unions Under the Combination Acts. 1799-1823.

Repeal of the Combination Acts. 1825.

Trade Unions in the Early 1830s. 1831-1837.

[Tufnell, Edward Carlton]
Character, Object and Effects of Trades' Unions; With Some Remarks on the Law Concerning Them. 1834.

Rebirth of the Trade Union Movement. 1838-1847.

Labour Disputes in the Mines. 1831-1844.

The Framework Knitters and Handloom Weavers; Their Attempts to Keep Up Wages. 1820-1845.

Robert Owen at New Lanark. 1824-1838.

Motherwell and Orbiston: The First Owenite Attempts at Cooperative Communities. 1822-1825.

Owenism and the Working Class. 1821-1834.

Cooperation and the Working Class: Theoretical Contributions. 1827-1834.

The Rational System. 1837-1841.

Cooperative Communities: Plans and Descriptions. 1825-1847.

The Factory Act of 1819. 1818-1819.

The Ten Hours Movement in 1831 and 1832. 1831-1832.

The Factory Act of 1833. 1833-1834.

Richard Oastler: King of Factory Children. 1835-1861.

The Battle for the Ten Hours Day Continues. 1837-1843.

The Factory Education Bill of 1843. 1843.

Prelude to Victory of the Ten Hours Movement. 1844.

Sunday Work. 1794-1856.

Demands for Early Closing Hours. 1843.

Conditions of Work and Living: The Reawakening of the English Conscience. 1838-1844.

Improving the Lot of the Chimney Sweeps. 1785-1840.

The Rising of the Agricultural Labourers. 1830-1831.

The Aftermath of the "Lost Labourers' Revolt". 1830-1831.